Folklore of the
Winnebago Tribe

FOLKLORE
OF THE
WINNEBAGO
TRIBE

By David Lee Smith

Foreword by Robert Conley

University of Oklahoma Press
Norman

Library of Congress
Cataloging-in-Publication Data

Smith, David Lee, 1950–
  Folklore of the Winnebago tribe /
  by David Lee Smith :
  foreword by Robert Conley.
      p.   cm.
  ISBN 978-0-8061-2976-1 (cloth)
  ISBN 978-0-8061-6471-7 (paper)

  1. Winnebago Indians—Folklore.
  2. Winnebago mythology.
  3. Legends—Wisconsin.
  I. Title.
  E99.W7S56   1997
  398.2 '089975—dc21   97-21663
                             CIP

The paper in this book meets
the guidelines for permanence
and durability of the Committee
on Production Guidelines for Book
Longevity of the Council on Library
Resources, Inc. ∞

Contents

v

Foreword

Tales from an oral tradition express the heart and soul of a people. They reveal the worldview of the people from whose tradition they arose. They explain how things came to be and why things are done the way they are, and they teach lessons of life. They also, of course, form the basis for the entire, continuing literature of a people.

Many collections of tales from Native American tribal oral traditions have been published. Too often, however, they are presented as something other than what they are or for reasons completely beyond their reason for being.

Some tales, singly or in collections, are presented as children's stories only. Others, in anthologies made up of a scattering of tales from various tribes, seem to present us with collections of quaint curiosities, much like artifacts in a museum display case. Some collections seem to exist solely as raw material for the analytical mind of the non-Indian anthropologist or ethnologist to use as something to pile his pedantic observations around.

This collection of Winnebago tales compiled and edited by David Lee Smith, Winnebago tribal historian, is unique. First of all, it is entirely Winnebago. (A few of the tales, duly noted, were originally collected and published in another context by non-Indian scholars.) The book's purpose, organization, and structure are clearly explained in straightforward and readable introductory material. Although David Smith is a more than capable scholar with sound academic credentials, he has here wisely dispensed with anthropological, ethnological, or any other kind of academic jargon to make his text easily and comfortably accessible to the average reader. David has included in the collection contemporary tales written in the traditional manner by Winnebago students, thereby dramatically illustrating the too-often-overlooked fact that the tradition is alive. The culture is vital. All is continual and ongoing. American Indians exist in the present, not just in the past, and should be written about in the present as well as the past tense.

Because of the skillful combination of logically arranged tales and explanatory historical and cultural material, I can think of no other single book that would present either the casual reader or the serious scholar with a better introduction to or overall understanding of Winnebago people and culture than this one.

Once upon a time at Morningside College in Sioux City, Iowa, David Smith was a student of mine. He has since gone well beyond that to become a scholar whose work I admire. He is and always will be a friend of mine, and I am pleased and proud that he has given me the opportunity to write this foreword. This book is one of which David and the Winnebago people can be proud and from which the rest of us can derive wisdom, knowledge, and joy. Putting the oral tradition into print is not ever an easy task. David Smith has done an admirable job of that, giving us in the process a book that is both worthwhile and a pleasure to read. What more can we ask?

ROBERT J. CONLEY
Cherokee

Tahlequah, Oklahoma

Acknowledgments

I received my first training in storytelling from my late father, Waukon G. Smith. He passed to the Spiritland in 1991. Some of my stories come from my mother, Mrs. Emily Lowry Smith, and my storytelling mentor, Dr. Felix White, Sr. Others are from my Winnebago community college students. Fourteen of the stories are my own.

Some stories in the text were collected by others in years past. Paul Radin collected a lot of Winnebago material from 1906 to 1920. W. C. McKern collected his stories from the Winnebagos of Wisconsin in the 1920s and 1930s. Oliver LaMere, a Winnebago graduate of Carlisle Indian School (1879–1918), and Joseph LaMere, a graduate of Hampton Indian School (1878–1923), wrote stories for various publications around the turn of the century. The sources of the stories are noted in the text. To all my people, the ones who went to the Spiritland and the ones living on Turtle Island, I want to say thank you.

In more detail I want to thank various publishing organizations and my Winnebago students for granting me permission to use their stories.

In particular, I want to thank the following elders: Emily L. Smith, for "Ma-ona and the Creation of the World," Felix White, Sr., for "Origin Story of the Winnebago Clans" and "Origin of the Winnebago Chief," and Waukon G.

Smith, for "Origin Story of Lake Winnebago, Wisconsin" and "Wak'djunk'aga the Eagle."

Others to whom I express thanks are Ilona Maney, Dawn Makes Strong Move, Pat Medina, Rita Sharpback, Keely Bassette, Jennifer Smith, and Joi St. Cyr. For details, see the list of contents. Ilona Maney and Rita Sharpback are employed at the Winn-A-Vegas Casino for the Winnebago Tribe of Nebraska. Dawn Makes Strong Move is working on her master's degree at the University of Connecticut. Patricia Medina is working on her master's at Morningside College, and Joi St. Cyr is completing her bachelor's degree. Jennifer Smith works as a teacher for the Winnebago tribal Head Start program, and Keely Bassette works for the Winnebago Tribe in its tribal headquarters in the town of Winnebago.

I thank the American Anthropological Association for Paul Radin's "Winnebago Tales," published in the *Journal of American Folklore* 22 (1909), 88-101. The tales include Sam Blowsnake's "The Origin of the Thunderbird Clan and of Their Spirit Abode," Joseph LaMere's "The Man Who Visited the Thunderbirds" and "The Orphan Boy Who Was Captured by the Bad Thunderbirds," Soloman Longtail's "How the Two Divisions of the Winnebago Came Together," and Ruth Benedict, ed., "Some Representative Tales and Myths." Paul Radin's "Turtle Trying to Get Credit, a Tale," first appeared in *Journal of American Folklore* 39 (1926), 27-52.

My thanks go to the Milwaukee Public Museum for W. C. McKern, "A Winnebago Myth," in the museum's *Yearbook* 9 (1929), 215-30. McKern's "Winnebago Dog Myths" appeared in *Yearbook* 10 (1930), 317-22. Thanks to the Wisconsin Archeological Society and the Wisconsin Archeologist for Oliver LaMere, "Winnebago Legends," published in *Wisconsin Archeologist* 21 (April 1922), 66-68. Also published by the Wisconsin Archeological Society were #4800 Dorsey Papers—Chiwere Texts, from the anthropological archives.

To the National Museum of Natural History at the Smithsonian Institution, Washington, D.C., thanks for Oliver LaMere, "The Rabbit and the Grasshoppers," Louis L. Meeker, "The Morning Star," and two stories by unknown authors, "The Story of Watekqua and His Brothers" and "The Captive Boys."

I also want to thank Lyn Broderson, of Sioux City, Iowa, and Karen Kemling, of the Little Priest Tribal College, who typed and edited the manuscript. Lyn Broderson did the first draft and Karen Kemling the later versions. Without their help, the manuscript would never have been completed.

Acknowledg-
ments

This book is dedicated to three remarkable women who were major influences on my life. My Lakota grandmother, Lucy, who passed into the spirit world in 1976 and who taught me to feel proud to be an American Indian; my mother, Emily, who backed my education at Morningside College and at UCLA; and Regina LittleBeaver, my big sister, who continuously gives me encouragement and support.

To these three Indian women, I say, thank you very much.

Folklore of the
Winnebago Tribe

Introduction

My name is David Lee Smith. I am a member of the Winnebago Tribe of Nebraska and currently the tribal historian. The Winnebago people are a Woodland tribe that was placed in the plains when most of the eastern tribes were moved west of the Mississippi in the removal era of the 1830s. During their movement out of Wisconsin to Nebraska between 1840 and 1865, the Winnebagos appear to have maintained a degree of cultural stability that is still present.

Probably no other tradition in Winnebago tribal culture explains the people better than their own oral tradition that many people call folklore. The stories in this book, which come from the Winnebago oral tradition, can be classified in four groups. The primary group is that of the origin story. Origin stories help to explain how the Creator came to exist, how he created the universe, and how he made the creatures who inhabited the planet Earth. When the Creator first put beings upon the earth, they all shared a common language. The two-legged and four-legged creatures, the birds, the insects, the fish, and even the trees could communicate using a lingua franca.

The second group of stories is made up of the trickster stories. The Winnebago trickster is commonly referred to as Wak'djunk'aga. He is a primitive, cosmic being of both divine and animal nature. On the one hand, he is superior to man by reason of his supernatural qualities. On the other, he is inferior to man by virtue of his extraordinary clumsiness and lack of awareness.* The function of the trickster is to teach humans to laugh at themselves. He is the shadow of the human. He embodies the inferior traits of character that humans all possess. He is the second personality trapped in each one of us. The Winnebagos traditionally have used these stories as teaching tools for the younger generation. Wak'djunk'aga could indeed prove to be a driving moral force in today's society.

The third group of stories encompasses the mythology of the Winnebago Tribe. A myth always attempts to explain something. Myths may, for example, explain the behavior of dogs, why ducks have red eyes, or where tobacco came from. Each myth relates to the world and the universe created by Ma-ona for the Winnebagos.

The last group of stories is the legend group. Tribal legends, like the other groups of stories, were handed down from the elders, generation after generation. They recount histories of war and migrations; they convey the history and customs of the Winnebago people. The legendary world of the Winnebagos is still alive today.

The material I gathered for this work comes from four kinds of fieldwork. First, I am an oral traditionalist. The stories that I relate have been handed down through untold generations in my family and clan. Each clan of the Winnebago Tribe has an oral traditionalist—a tradition still being practiced in the modern era. I can trace my family line back to 1640 through the Thunder Clan. There has been an oral traditionalist in my family since that time, and when I pass on to the Spiritland, a younger member of my family and

---

* The trickster Wak'djunk'aga was put on Earth at the start of the world by Ma-ona, the Winnebago tribal name for the Creator. He possesses both human and godlike qualities. Wak'djunk'aga not only laughs and cries like a human being, but he also has to sleep and eat. He is immortal and cannot die on Mother Earth. He was put on Earth by Ma-ona to get the Winnebagos and other Indians on the "right path of life." Only after he accomplishes this task will Wak'djunk'aga be called back to the heavens by the Creator.

clan will take up my stories and pass them on to another generation. This way of storytelling is not about to change even in these modern times.

The second kind of fieldwork that I use comes from Winnebago elders of different clans. Only one of them is still living today. The late Felix White, Sr., an oral traditionalist of the Wolf Clan, was my mentor from 1981. Emily L. Smith, my mother, is an oral traditionalist of the Bear Clan, and her story is still handed down in that clan. The late Waukon G. Smith, my father, came from a long line of traditional chiefs of the tribe. His stories are very old and come from a time when the Winnebagos were one of the few tribes in the state of Wisconsin.

The third group of informants who have contributed to this work are Winnebago people from around the turn of the twentieth century. Most of their stories were told to anthropologists and ethnologists at the time when Winnebagos still told their stories in their native tongue. When Native Americans relate their stories in their own tribal tongue, the full meaning of those stories comes out. When English is used in the storytelling, a story looks more like a fable to the non-Indian world, because some of the cultural context of the story is lost. Most of these stories were published in journals or placed in archival centers. For this book, some of the older stories have undergone minor editing.

The fourth group of informants are Winnebago students whom I have had in my classroom. Five of the students were born on the reservation and have lived here all their lives. Two of the students were born in the cities, but since then have returned to the Winnebago reservation. All of these students still practice the traditional dances, games, and belief systems of their respective clans. They all know the history of the tribe, as is evident in their stories. One cannot write stories unless one is somewhat versed in the tribe's customs and beliefs. As their teacher, I did not have to encourage my students to express themselves too much in their stories, because their talent lies just below the surface, waiting to be tapped.

Many modern Winnebagos express their culture without even knowing they are doing so. Some are artists, some are dancers, and some are singers. Many have traditional talents that are brought out by themselves in the way they do things. Pat Medina is a flute player. One has to know the culture, history, and traditions of the tribe in order to be a flute player, because each song is a story passed down through music. Ilona Maney and Joi St. Cyr are Bear Clan members who still practice the traditional dances of the tribe. Jennifer Smith tells stories in the same style that her mother Emily uses. Both are represented in this book. Rita Sharpback and Keely Bassette wrote their stories together to show how two generations can teach each other. Both women come from very traditional families. Dawn Makes Strong Moves comes from the city, as is evident in her story. She is trying to explain how the Winnebago trickster can fit into the modern world as a teaching tool for the younger generation.

Most of the stories these women tell come from their own creative efforts and beliefs. All are written from the Winnebago tribal point of view. That is how the tribal people express themselves in the modern world, while still using their own history, culture, and traditions. All the stories are quite similar to the stories of the past; there is family and clan influence in their stories. The only story that is told from a modern point of view is "Wak'djunk'aga and the Car," and even this story shows that Dawn Makes Strong Move is a student of Winnebago history and folklore.

Even with their own culture changing around them, the Winnebago people still maintain the rules of the clan system that was laid down for them hundreds of years ago. Their responsibilities to their respective clans have changed in the modern world, but the religious and spiritual aspect will never change among the Winnebago people. Clan names are still given out to the younger generation at ceremonies held throughout the year. Clan feasts are still given.

Some stories are seasonal. Oral traditionalists still tell certain stories in the wintertime as they have for centuries—

since before contact with the Europeans. Other stories are told throughout the year.

As the Winnebago tribal historian, I know that many of our tribal stories are centuries old, but that each new generation brings forth new stories to try to explain the world as it changes around them. In this way, the culture of the Winnebago people will continue through both the old and new stories.

There is a cultural awakening on the Nebraska Winnebago reservation today, and storytelling is again becoming part of every clan's traditions. As long as there is one Winnebago left in the world, storytelling will continue.

The Winnebago Tribe

The Winnebagos are a Siouan-speaking people who inhabited Wisconsin during the precontact period. The Winnebago Tribe entered Wisconsin from the southeast and north of Lake Michigan around A.D. 700. The Winnebagos referred to themselves as "Ho-chun-gra" or "Ho-Chunk," which translates as, "People of the parent speech."

The tribe's first encounter with Europeans was with French explorers in 1614, when a number of Winnebagos met Samuel de Champlain on the shores of Lake Superior. In 1634, Jean Nicolet met five thousand Winnebago warriors in the Green Bay area. At that time, the tribe's population was twenty-five thousand. Between 1634 and 1640, however, this number decreased dramatically due to three successive smallpox epidemics and warfare with surrounding Algonquian tribes.

The nucleus of the remaining tribal members forged an alliance with the French during the Beaver Wars (1667-1697) against the Iroquois. In 1702, the tribe shifted diplomatic association with the Europeans, joining the Fox Indian Alliance. This change in affiliation eventually led—in 1728—to the first schism of the Winnebagos.

In the latter part of the eighteenth century, the Winnebago Tribe again joined forces with the French, this time against the British during the French and Indian War (1755-1763). Winnebago diplomatic loyalties shifted once more when the tribe came to the aid of the British during the American Revolution (1776-1783). The tribe's affiliation with the British endured throughout the War of 1812, when the Winnebagos, along with Tecumseh's Indian Confederation, were defeated by U.S. forces.

The loss marked the final split within the tribe, and the Green Bay Winnebagos reluctantly signed their first treaty with the U.S. government in 1816. Three additional territorial treaties were negotiated and signed in 1825, 1827, and 1828. Subsequent treaties of land cessions were signed by the tribe in 1829, 1832, 1837, 1846, 1855, and 1859. In spite of Winnebago cooperation with the U.S. government, the tribe was removed from Wisconsin to "Neutral Ground" in Iowa in 1840, to the Long Prairie Reservation in Minnesota in 1846, to the Blue Earth Reservation in 1855, and finally to the Crow Creek, South Dakota Reservation in 1863. When part of the tribe died of starvation, the Winnebagos fled to the Omaha Reservation in 1864 to 1865. There, tribal leaders purchased land from the Omaha Tribe with funds acquired as a result of the Crow Creek cession.

During the Allotment Era (1887-1934), the Winnebago Tribe lost 75 percent of their newly procured reservation land. This loss contributed heavily to political turmoil within the tribe. As a result, 50 percent of the tribe returned to Wisconsin in order to organize a political unit independent of the Nebraska Winnebagos. The Winnebago Tribe of Nebraska reorganized, with elected tribal officials, under the 1934 Indian Reorganization Act government.

Today, the Nebraska Winnebagos number just over four thousand (an estimated 4,100) and the Wisconsin branch remains close to five thousand. Approximately one thousand Winnebagos reside in urban areas due to the termination policy of the 1950s, but the urban Winnebago populations still maintain close ties with their relatives in Nebraska and Wisconsin. Thus, in spite of several tribal schisms, the

Winnebago Tribe persists as a strong and viable part of Native American society.

The Clan System

The Winnebago Tribe organized itself into two major divisions: the Sky Clans and the Earth Clans. There were four Sky Clans—the Thunder Clan, Hawk Clan, Eagle Clan, and Pigeon Clan. The Earth Clans were eight in number— the Bear Clan, Wolf Clan, Water-Spirit Clan, Deer Clan, Elk Clan, Buffalo Clan, Fish Clan, and Snake Clan.

All twelve clans cooperated in tribal affairs, each clan having particular responsibilities for an aspect of Winnebago life. The Thunder Clan supplied the civil leaders of the tribe. The Hawk Clan were soldiers, authorized to decree life-and-death decisions when captives were taken in war. The Eagle and Pigeon Clans supplied soldiers for warfare and hunting. The Bear Clan were the police officers and the Wolf Clan performed social welfare roles, administering public health and safety. The Water-Spirit Clan protected the water supply. The Deer Clan's responsibilities concerned the environment and weather. The Elk Clan's functions were related to the distribution of fire through the village, the hunt, and on the warpath. The Buffalo Clan were town criers to the chief. The Fish Clan supplied soldiers for warfare and helped take care of the village. The Snake Clan dealt with sanitation and kept watch as listeners for intruders. In warfare, the Snake and Fish Clans formed the first line of defense.

A special bond existed between certain clans. These "friendship relations" paired off clans as follows: Thunder with Hawk, Eagle with Pigeon, Bear with Wolf, Buffalo with Water-Spirit, Elk with Deer, and Fish with Snake. Friendship relations provided for mutual service between clans on four specific occasions. If a member of a clan visited a friendship relation, the relation was obligated to perform various services, such as feeding and sheltering the guest for the evening. Clans also sought revenge for injustices committed against the friendship relation. The friendship relation could be called upon to lend a clan name to an individual being honored in a naming feast. And friendship relations always arranged the burial of members of the friendship clan.

Most of the responsibilities of the clans have changed in the modern world, but Winnebago tribal people still maintain close clan ties with each other and their friendship clan. The bond that has united people is still in place after years of reservation life.

The Season When the Winnebagos Told Their Stories

Among the Winnebagos, the winter season was the time for the telling of myths and legends of the tribe—a tradition continued to this day. The stories were usually told on a cold winter night, when the wind blew fiercely from the north across the prairie. This was the time, in the early days, when Winnebago families and close friends gathered in the family wigwam around the fire to listen to elders versed in the stories of the tribe.

The Winnebago storytellers refused to tell their stories at any other time of the year, because according to legend the Ice Giants always lurked about the camp during the winter. The Ice Giants were very strong and they were always searching for Winnebago victims to fill their food kettles. If a member of the tribe encountered one of these cannibalistic Ice Giants, there was no escape.

The Winnebagos occasionally offered the Ice Giants tobacco, feathers, and food to keep them away from family dwellings. When the gifts were offered in the early evening, the sacred myths and legends were recited well into the night.

Many of these beliefs are still practiced by contemporary Winnebagos, but the storytelling is done in a house, not a wigwam.

DAVID LEE SMITH
Winnebago Tribal Historian
Winnebago Tribe of Nebraska

Part One

CREATION STORIES

Ma-ona
and the
Creation
of the World

By Emily L. Smith, Bear Clan

Ma-ona the Creator awakened.* He thought of the substance upon which he was sitting. He saw nothing. There was nothing but empty space everywhere. Ma-ona cried. Then the Creator took some of the substance upon which he was sitting. He rolled it up into a ball. Ma-ona then cast it down from the heavens upon which he sat. Then he looked down upon it. Nothing grew upon it. It was lifeless, bare, and very quiet.

The ball kept turning round and round and round. Then Ma-ona made the first Winnebago man. He called him Turtle. Then Ma-ona made other men, and then he made women. Ma-ona smiled to himself, because his people looked very good. Ma-ona then told Turtle of all that he had created.

He sent Turtle down to make the world a safe place to live. Turtle found the people to be too happy, though, so he made them start fighting each other. There were battles all over the world. Ma-ona felt bad, so he called Turtle back to the heavens.

He next sent Rabbit down to earth to restore order, but Rabbit did a very bad thing. He gave humans life immortal. He then killed the spirits who were terrorizing humankind.

As related to David Lee Smith in an interview.

*Ma-ona and Earth-Maker are the same person in the cosmology of the Winnebago Tribe. He is the Creator, the maker of all things in the universe.

Rabbit's grandmother became very angry at her grandson Rabbit because he made humans immortal. She said, "Ma-ona, the Creator, made death so there should be no lack of food in the world. He created death to prevent overcrowding. The Creator provided a spirit world for humans to stay in after their earthly existence came to an end."

Grandmother told Rabbit to walk ahead of her while she followed him. She told her grandson to look ahead and never look back. They commenced a walk around the world. Halfway through the journey, Rabbit could stand his curiosity no longer. He turned his head to look behind him, and as he did so, the world came crashing in upon itself. Rabbit's curiosity brought death back to Ma-ona's world.*

---

*In the cosmology of the Winnebago people, the Creator made Wak'djunk'aga the Trickster, Turtle, Red Horn, and the Hare. Rabbit was brother to the Hare. These creations of Ma-ona are supernatural beings. They can take both human and animal forms, and were sent by the creator at the beginning of the world to help mankind in various ways. One way was to get mankind on the right path to life.

Origin Story
of the
Winnebago Clans

By Felix White, Sr., Wolf Clan

In the beginning, Ma-ona the Creator surveyed the world he had created. He noticed some beings who walked on two legs, but they were walking with great difficulty. Soon Ma-ona saw enormous monsters devouring the two-legged beings. Many two-legged beings went mad after seeing their brothers and sisters eaten by these fiends. Such a sight upset Ma-ona greatly, so he called twelve beings who had wings and asked them to perform as overseers for the two-legged beings. Ma-ona was busy with other things and could not attend to his creation.

Ma-ona was very proud of what he had made. Four of the winged beings flew in the air to look down upon the earth to observe the monsters' atrocities. The four winged beings became known as the Sky People: Thunder, Eagle, Hawk, and Pigeon. The remaining eight winged creatures became Bear, Wolf, Water-Spirit, Deer, Elk, Buffalo, Fish, and Snake—the Earth People. Ma-ona decided to make the Earth and Sky People equal; he refused to make one of them leader of all others. The Earth and Sky People queried of themselves, "Which language will we speak together?" The eldest of the twelve, Thunder, replied, "We will speak Ho-Chunk." *Chunk* is a word meaning praise. The elder had encouraged the beings to speak their language in praise of the Creator. Ho-Chunk would become the voice of praise.

As related to David Lee Smith in an interview.

None of the beings asked to serve as chief. The clans instead would follow the plan of Ma-ona; and organize themselves into equal entities. As a result of the cooperation of the twelve clans, the Winnebago Tribe functioned as a harmonious whole composed of different parts.

Origin of the
Winnebago Chief

By Felix White, Sr., Wolf Clan

Long ago, the Winnebagos met to elect a chief. Prior to the meeting, the tribe only recognized clan leaders. Twelve clans formed the backbone of the Winnebago Tribe. They were called Thunder, Eagle, Hawk, Pigeon, Bear, Wolf, Water-Spirit, Deer, Elk, Buffalo, Fish, and Snake. The twelve clans formed a Grand National Council, and decided to have an athletic contest to decide who the council's leader would be.

Thunder, Eagle, and Hawk thought that they would win the race because they were all swift and experienced in flight. They were confident because no earth animal had ever defeated them. Pigeon, who was swift yet modest, won the race around the world. Pigeon, however, did not desire the title.

They raced again. This time Elk won the race. Elk renounced his title in favor of his uncle, Eagle. The Eagle Clan then gained chieftainship of the Winnebago Tribe, but Thunder intervened. He said, "My clan is the highest, and I should be chief." Some of the other clans supported Thunder, so he became chief. The Eagle Clan was demoted to second place in the Sky Clans. That is how the Thunder Clan won the chieftainship of the Winnebago Tribe.

As related to David Lee Smith in an interview.

17

The Origin of the
Thunderbird Clan
and of
Their Spirit Abode

By Samuel Blowsnake, Snake Clan

In the beginning, Earth-Maker was sitting in space, when he came to consciousness, and nothing else was there, anywhere. He began to think of what he should do, and finally he began to cry. Tears began to flow from his eyes and fall down below him. After a while he looked below him and saw something bright. The bright objects were his tears that flowed below and formed the present waters.

When the tears flowed below, they became the seas as they are now. Earth-Maker began to think again. He thought, "It is thus, if I wish anything, it will become as I wish, just as my tears have become seas." Thus he thought.

So he wished for light, and it became light. Then he thought, "It is as I supposed, the things that I wished for came into existence as I desired." Then he again thought and wished for the earth, and this earth came into existence. Earth-Maker looked on the earth, and he liked it, but it was not quiet. It moved about as do the waves of the seas. Then he made the trees, and he saw that they were good, but they did not make the earth quiet. Then he made the grass grow, but the earth was not quiet yet. Then he made the rocks and stones, but still the earth was not quiet. However, it was nearly quiet.

Then he made the four directions (cardinal points) and the four winds. On the four corners of the earth he placed

---

Story collected by David Lee Smith.

18

them as great and powerful people, to act as island weights. Yet the earth was not quiet. Then he made four large beings and threw them down toward the earth, and they pierced through the earth with their heads eastward. They were snakes. Then the earth became very still and quiet. Then he looked upon the earth, and he saw that it was good.

Then he thought again of how things came into existence just as he desired. Then he first began to talk. He said, "As things become just as I wish them, I shall make one in my own likeness." So he took a piece of clay (earth) and made it like himself. Then he talked to what he had created, but it did not answer. He looked upon it, and saw that it had no mind or thought, so he made a mind for it. Again he talked to it, but it did not answer. He looked upon it again, and saw that it had no tongue. Then he made it a tongue. He talked to it again, but it did not answer. He looked upon it, and he saw that it had no soul; so he made it a soul. He talked to it again, and this time it very nearly said something. But it did not make itself intelligible, so Earth-Maker breathed into its mouth and talked to it, and it answered.

As the newly created being was in his own likeness, Earth-Maker felt quite proud of him, so he made three more just like him. He made them powerful, so that they might watch over the earth. These first four he made chiefs of the Thunderbirds; and he thought, "Some will I make to live upon the earth that I have made." So he made four more beings in his own likeness. Just like the others he made them. They were brothers, Ku'nuga, Hay'na-ga, Ha-ga-ga and Na-yi'ga.

He talked to them and said, "Look down upon the earth." So saying, he opened the heavens in front of where they sat and there they saw the earth (spread out below them). He told them that they were to go down there to live. "And this I shall send with you," he added, and he gave them a plant. "I, myself, shall not have any power to take this from you, as I have given it to you; but when, of your own free will, you make me an offering of some of it, I shall gladly accept it and give what you ask. This shall you hold foremost in your lives." It was a tobacco plant that he had given them.

He said also, "All the spirits that I create will not be able to take this from you unless you desire to give it by calling upon them during fasts and offering it to them. Thus only can the spirits get any of it. And this also I send with you, that you may use it in life. When you offer anything, it shall be your mediator. It shall take care of you through life. It shall stand in the center of your dwellings, and it shall be your grandfather." Thus he spoke to them. What he meant was the fire. Then he gave them the earth to live on. So the four Thunder-spirits brought the four brothers down to the earth. The oldest one, Ku'nuga, said while on their way down, "Brothers, when we get to the earth and the first child is born to me, I shall call him 'King (chief) of the Thunders,' if it be a boy." On they came, down toward the earth. When they got near the earth, it began to get very dark.

Then the second brother said, "Brothers, when we get to the earth and a child is born to me, if it is a girl, it shall be called 'Dark.'" They came to a place called Within-Lake-at-Red-Banks, a lake near Green Bay. On an oak tree south of the lake is the place where they alighted. The branch they alighted on bent down from their weight. Then said the third brother to his brothers, "The first daughter born to me shall be called, 'She-Who-Weighs-the-Tree-Down-Woman.'" They alighted on earth, but the Thunder-spirits did not touch the earth. Then said the fourth and last brother to his brothers, "Brothers, the first son that is born to me shall be called, 'He-Who-Alights-on-the-Earth.'" The first thing they did on earth was to start their fire.

Then Earth-Maker looked down upon them and saw that he had not prepared any food for them, so he made the animals, that they might have something to eat. The oldest brother said, "What are we going to eat?" Then the youngest two took the bow and arrows that Earth-Maker had given them, and started toward the east. Not long after, the third brother came into view with a young deer on his back, and the youngest brother also came with a young deer about two years old on his back.

The deer that were killed were brothers, and those that killed them were also brothers. They were very much delighted that they had obtained food. Then said they, "Let us give our grandfather the first taste." Saying thus, they cut off the ends of the tongues and the heart and threw them into the fire with some fat.

The first people to call on them were the War People. They came from the west. Then came four others. They were the Thunders. Thus they were called, the youngest brothers. Then came those of the earth. Then came those of the Deer Clan. Then came those of the Bear Clan. Then came those of the Fish Clan. Then came those of the Water-Spirit Clan, and all the other clans that exist.

Then there appeared on the lake a very white bird, Swan they called it; and after that, all the other water birds that exist came. And they named them in the order of their coming, until the lake was quite full. Then the people began to dress the deer meat. Suddenly something came and alighted on the deer meat. "What is that?" they said. Then said Ku'nuga, the oldest brother, "It is a wasp; and the first dog that I possess, if it is black, 'Wasp' I shall call it." Thus he spoke, "And as the wasp scented and knew of the deer dressing, so shall the dog be toward other animals; and wherever the dog is and animals are in the windward, he shall scent them."

They made a feast with the deer for Earth-Maker and threw tobacco into the fire and offered it to him. And to the other clans they showed how fire was to be made, and gave them some. "For," they said, "each of you must now make fire for yourselves, as we shall not always lend you some." There the people made their home. It was just the time of the year when the grass comes as far as the knee (summer).

One day they reported that something very strange was near the camp, but they said to themselves, "We will leave it alone." In a little while it moved nearer. Thus it moved toward the camp, and soon it began to eat deer bones. They allowed it to become one of the clans, and took it into their house. It was the dog, or wolf. They killed one of them, and made a feast to Earth-Maker, telling him all about what they had done.

In the beginning the Thunder Clanspeople were as powerful as the thunder-spirits themselves. It was the Thunder People who made the ravines and valleys. While wandering around the world, the Thunder People struck the earth with their clubs and made dents in the hills. That is the reason that the upper clans are chiefs of all the others, and that the least of all are the Dog People. So it was.

One day the oldest of the brothers lay down and did not rise again, and he did not breathe, and he became cold. "What is the matter with our oldest brother?" the three others said. Four days they waited for him, but still he did not arise. So the second brother was asked by his youngest brother what the trouble was. He did not know anything about it and told him to ask his third brother. The third brother did not know either. Then the two older brothers asked the youngest one, but he did not know either. So they began to mourn for the older brother, not knowing what to do or think.

They fasted and blackened their faces, as we do now when we are mourning. They made a platform and laid him on it. When the snow fell knee deep, the three brothers filled their pipe and went toward the place of the coming of the daylight, the east. There they came to the first being that Earth-Maker had placed in the east, the Island Weight, as he was called. They came to him weeping, and went into his tent, turning the stem of their pipe in his mouth. They said, "Grandfather, our brother Ku'nuga has fallen and is not able to rise again. Earth-Maker made you great, and endowed you with all knowledge, and thus you know all things."

He answered and said, "My dear grandsons, I am sorry I do not know anything about it, but as you have started to find out, I would refer you to the one ahead of me (the north). Perhaps North can tell you.

So weeping, they started for the next one. When they got to North and told him their troubles, he told them he could not help them. "But," he said, "perhaps the one ahead of me knows." So they started for the third one (the west), but from him likewise they could learn nothing. West also referred them to the one ahead (the south). When they reached the fourth and last one, they entered the lodge, and behold, there sat the three to whom they had gone before.

Here they asked the last one for help; not only he, but the other three also answered them, "Grandsons, thus Earth-Maker has willed it. Your brother will not rise again. He will be with you no more in this world. And as long as this world lasts, so it will be with human beings. Whenever one reaches the age of death, one shall die, and those that wish to live long will have to attain that age by good actions. Thus they will live long. Into your bodies Earth-Maker has placed part of himself. That will return to him if you do the proper things. This world will come to an end some time. Your brother shall keep a village in the west for all the souls of your clan, and there he shall be in full charge of all of you. And when this world is ended, your brother shall take all the souls back to Earth-Maker; at least, all those who have acted properly. Thus it was. Now you may go home and bury your brother in the proper manner."

The Thunder People thanked the four spirits and left the tent. When they got home they took their brother's body, dressed him in his best clothes, and painted his face. Then they told him where he was to go and buried him with his head toward the west, and with his war club. They placed the branch of a tree at his grave and painted a little stick red and tied it to the tree, so that nothing should cross his path on his journey to the spirit abode. If any thing or animal should cross his path on that journey, he must strike it with his club and throw it behind him, so that those relatives he has left behind on earth might derive blessings in war and attain long life. He would have his pipe and food along with him on his journey, and thus the things that he throws behind him will be a blessing for those still remaining on earth. Also the life he leaves behind him, (that is to say, the years that had he lived to a normal age, are still due him) and the victories that he might have gained—all these he is to give to his relatives. The riches he might have had—or, in fact, anything that he could possibly have had—he is asked to give to these relatives. Then they will not feel so unhappy and lonesome. Such is the story up to the time that the spirit starts on his journey to the Spiritland.

The Winnebagos always encouraged one another to die on the warpath because, if one dies in battle, the person would really not lose consciousness but simply live right on in the spirit, and death would seem to him as if he had stumbled over some object. So they would say, if you wish to live a happy life as a spirit, do not die in your house. If you die in your house, your soul will wander all over the earth in want, and when people eat at the four-nights' wake, you will not get anything. If they drink water, you will remain thirsty.

It is said that people not dying on the warpath will, as spirits, have to content themselves by pointing to food and drink and licking their fingers. Those that die in battle have a village four days' distance from the general village of the souls. They are in need of nothing, as they plant and raise their own food, and have so many clothes that they look as if they were covered with furs. They play ball and have lots of fun, ride horseback, and dance. If any of them should desire to return to the earth and become alive again, they can do so.

The wounds, however, from which they died, remain with them in the spirit world. Those who lost their scalps are without scalps. Some are without heads and some are without scalplocks. They can see their relatives here on earth whenever they wish to. So the people encouraged one another to die bravely and on the warpath.

Origin Story of Lake Winnebago, Wisconsin

By Waukon G. Smith, Thunder Clan

One day in the woods, Wak'djunk'aga, the Winnebago trickster, was talking to Brother Bear. "Brother Bear," he said, "do you think I can see Ma-ona the Creator?"

"Sure," said Brother Bear, "but you have to die first."

So Wak'djunk'aga went to a village where the warriors were shooting arrows. He cried out, "Shoot me! Shoot me! I bet you can't hit me!"

They shot him full of holes, but he could not die. Wak'djunk'aga now felt especially sad because he could not see Ma-ona. So he went to the top of a cliff and cried and cried until his tears formed a large lake. Lake Winnebago is the creation of Wak'djunk'aga's tears.*

As related to David Lee Smith in an interview.

*This origin story dates back to when the Winnebagos first moved to Wisconsin. Ma-ona sent Wak'djunk'aga to earth to help humans and he could not leave until orderly life was established. Wak'djunk'aga was not ready to travel to the Spiritland. For this reason, he could not visit the Creator.

The Migration
of the
Ho-Chunk People

By David Lee Smith, Thunder Clan

According to various accounts, there were five Siouan migrations out of Kentucky and the southeast around A.D. 200.* The first of these were the people of the Mandan, Hidatsa, and Crow. They traveled northwest and settled in North Dakota and Montana. The second migration consisted of the Chiwere people, the Ho-Chunk, and their sister tribes—that is, the Oto, Iowa, and Missiouria. They traveled north toward the land of the lakes. The third group to leave was the Dhegiha people, consisting of the Omaha, Osage, Kansa, Ponca, and Quapaw.

These tribes traveled north to the Ohio River. From there, they went west, until they reached the mighty waters of the Mississippi. The Omaha and Ponca went down the Mississippi and up the Missouri River, while the rest journeyed to the Plains. The next peoples to leave Kentucky were the Lakota, Nakota, Dakota, and Assiniboine. They went northwest into Minnesota and later to the prairies, leaving the Dakota people among the pines. The last people to leave were the eastern people. They journeyed east over the mountains into Virginia and North Carolina. All these journeys occurred over hundreds of years.

I have discovered how things happened long ago by studying the Siouan legends and performing my own

*See George Hyde, *Indians of the Woodlands, from Prehistoric Times to 1725*, Norman: University of Oklahoma Press, 1962: 7–14; and Paul Radin, *Winnebago Tribe*, Lincoln: University of Nebraska Press, 1970: 1–4.

research.* The following legend helps to explain the Ho-Chunk migration.

One night, the Great Spirit appeared to Bear in a dream. "My son," he said, "it is time to leave your home and go to the new home that I have made for you. No longer will you eat solely from the water. There will be other food that I have put there for you to eat." So Bear called a council with all the other animals, including Wolf, Deer, Eagle, and Buffalo.

It was decided that Deer would lead the way, so he and his people left first. Bear and his people left in the second group, followed by Wolf in the third group. Buffalo left the next morning. The final animal to leave was the mighty Eagle. Before he departed, he blessed the people who were left behind. Eagle then flew into the sunrise and disappeared over the mountains. The spirits of the early people watched them leave with tears in their eyes, but happiness in their hearts.

After many passings of the moon, Bear and his people found a large river. There they held council, and it was decided that Turtle would carry them to the bank on the other side. While the earth animals rode on Turtle's back, the air animals flew overhead. These animals and all other animals would soon be known as the People of the Turtle. So it was back then, and so it is today.

Thus we see that linguistic, archaeological, and historical information obviously corresponds with Native American tradition and folklore.* If we continue to pray to the Great Spirit, we once more will become one people. The circle then will be complete.

27

The Migration of the Ho-Chunk People

---

*The Ho-Chunk migration legend was passed down to me years ago by elders of the Thunder Clan. See also the Dorsey Papers, 4800, Notes on Siouan Migrations 1–6, Anthropological Institution; and Amy E. Harvey, "Oneota Culture in Northwest Iowa," Iowa City: Office of the State Archeologist. University of Iowa. Report 12, 1970: 45–61.

†Many elders of related Siouan tribes whom I interviewed asked me to leave their names out of the manuscript. I did so to protect their privacy.

The Origin
of the
Big Dipper
and Little Dipper

By David Lee Smith, Thunder Clan

Once long ago, when the Winnebagos lived among the lakes, seven young women were chosen by the Creator himself to look after the sacred plants and herbs of the tribe. Seven young warriors were also chosen to be the protectors of these maidens throughout their lives. The Creator Ma-ona wanted these women pure and not to be touched by man.

One day the medicine woman of the tribe sent these young women on an herb-finding mission into the woods. They were to bring back medicinal plants needed by her for the treatment of the sick. The young warriors followed at a distance, but always keeping in eye contact with the women. Unknown to the warriors, they in turn were followed by an evil shaman of the hated Snake Tribe. He wanted the Winnebago virgins to be offered up as human sacrifices to his evil god.

When the seven maidens reached their favorite spot, they began picking the sacred plants needed by the medicine woman. Their activity was interrupted, however, when they were approached by a very handsome man. Unknown to them, this was the evil shaman (he could change his looks at will). All seven maidens fell in love with the handsome man at first sight, but they knew it was forbidden. So they all ran back to the village as quickly as their legs would carry them. They reported to the medicine woman what had happened.

The medicine woman became furious at the young warriors for not doing their duty. The leader of the young men said that at no time had they let the seven young women out of their sight. He said his group of warriors must have been bewitched. The medicine woman did not believe the leader, because she knew how young men were. So the next day, she again sent the maidens out and gave strict orders to the warriors not to let the women out of their sight.

As happened the day before, the evil shaman followed the maidens and their protectors at a distance. When the women reached their destination, again they started to pick the plants. The evil shaman then threw a veil of evil mist in front of the men's eyes so that they saw what he wanted them to see, which was a view of the women picking plants. As before, he again appeared to the women. This time he was even more handsome than before.

Now the maidens knew what he was. They all took off running, but could not find the trail back to their village. The evil shaman threw mist in front of them to confuse the young women. They then changed direction and ran toward the east, as the shaman wanted them to. Now there was no escape, for the lake was in front of them and the shaman was behind them.

After running for hours, the maidens began to tire and the evil one began to make up the distance between them. In the early hours of the evening, the women made it to the lake, just as the evil one caught up with them. Now he showed his true self to them, which was a demon god of the Snake people. The women now knew there was no escape, so they cried in one voice to the Creator, "Ma-ona! Help us, the demon is going to kill us and make food of our flesh!"

With a loud thundering of the heavens, Ma-ona answered their call. With a zap of lightning, the evil one was burned to a cinder, and the seven maidens were lifted up into the heavens and placed in the northwest. They became the Big Dipper. The evil shaman was placed as the North Star, so now the seven maidens could circle him and taunt him for eternity. The medicine woman of the Winnebagos threw the seven young warriors also into the heavens. They became the

Little Dipper. That was their payment for failing to protect Ma-ona's daughters.

To this day, in the early hours of darkness, you can see the seven maidens taunting the North Star, and their protectors in the Little Dipper forever keeping a watchful eye out for them.

Folklore
of the
Winnebago
Tribe

Part Two

TRICKSTER STORIES

Wak'djunk'aga
the Eagle

By Waukon G. Smith, Thunder Clan

One day as Wak'djunk'aga, the Winnebago trickster, was walking in the woods, he called his friends to join him. He called to Brother Rabbit, Brother Coyote, and Brother Squirrel, and they all came running to their friend. He told them, "Let us go up to that high cliff and look at the beautiful country."

As they traveled along, Rabbit ran and hopped high off the ground. Coyote sneaked slowly along. Squirrel climbed up and down the trees. Seeing his friends enjoying themselves, Wak'djunk'aga commented, "Brother Coyote, how I wish I could sneak along the ground like you!"

"You can sneak as I, if you only try." replied Brother Coyote.

As the friends continued on their journey, Wak'djunk'aga spoke to Brother Squirrel, "Brother Squirrel, how I wish I could climb up and down the trees like you!"

Answered Brother Squirrel, "You can! You can! If only you try!"

Looking at the sky, Wak'djunk'aga saw an eagle flying around a high cliff, and he noticed young eagles learning to fly and sail as well. He screamed to Sister Eagle, "How I wish I could fly and sail as you can!"

"You can and I will teach you," replied Sister Eagle.

As related to David Lee Smith in an interview.

As Sister Eagle and Wak'djunk'aga approached the top of the cliff, she explained to the trickster how he could fly, "Wak'djunk'aga, jump off the cliff. As you do so wave your arms very quickly, and then hold them out as I showed you earlier."

So, raising his arms, Wak'djunk'aga the trickster jumped, but he fell straight down, wildly flapping his arms, and hit the ground with a smashing blow. Sister Eagle lit next to him on the ground and said, "If Ma-ona wanted you to fly, he would have given you feathers, wings, and a tail!"

Moral: Never try to be something you are not. You should never brag, be conceited, or demand that which you do not deserve. Live with deep pride and self-confidence in your existence as a Native American and as an individual.

Folklore
of the
Winnebago
Tribe

Wak'djunk'aga
and Marriage

By David Lee Smith, Thunder Clan

One day in the spring, Wak'djunk'aga was sitting by the lake with Brother Deer. He said, "Brother Deer, today when I was coming along the path, I saw all my friends with women, and they told me they had married." He continued, "How come I can't get married?"

Deer spoke, "Wak'djunk'aga, you're in luck! Sister Bear wants to marry someone." So it came to pass, Wak'djunk'aga was married.

On their wedding night, while making love, Sister Bear accidentally scratched Wak'djunk'aga. "Yeeow!" he screamed. "You big-nosed Hun'ta, you hurt me!" Wak'djunk'aga struck Sister Bear. In return, she opened her mouth and bit his head off.

So, when you marry, be careful to avoid arguments with your mate. If you do, he or she won't bite you. If more people today followed this example, there wouldn't be so many divorces. The married couple must always respect each other.

The
Trickster
and Red Ant

By Pat Smith Medina, Thunder Clan

The trickster was sitting in the grass when his friend Red Ant came along. Red-Ant asked Trickster to come with him to gather honey. Trickster said, "I will help you gather honey if you promise to let me have my share."

Red-Ant said, "I will let you have your share, Trickster. You may eat first."

Trickster was very proud of himself for persuading Red Ant. He thought quietly that Red-Ant must have been quite hungry to agree to such conditions. Trickster continued, "After I eat all the honey, there will be only a few drops left for Red-Ant."

As they approached the beehive, Red-Ant said, "There it is, my friend. You go first. Don't forget to call me when you have had your share."

Trickster laughed to himself and said, "I will do just that, Red-Ant."

Trickster put his head inside the beehive. Suddenly, hundreds of bees began to sting him. He ran as fast as he could and cried out for help, "Red-Ant!"

"Thank you for calling me, my friend. I can see that you have had your share," replied Red-Ant.

Wak'djunk'aga
Learns a Lesson
in Niceness

By Rita Sharpback, Buffalo Clan,
and Keely Bassette, Water Spirit Clan

One day, He-nu Rabbit moved to a new town and had to start at a new school. After she got her new locker number, she went to find it. She had a locker next to Wak'djunk'aga. He was surrounded by friends, and when he saw the new girl, He-nu Rabbit, he started to make fun of her because her hair, clothes, and features were different than everyone else's. Because of the way He-nu Rabbit was raised, she held her tongue and said nothing. Wak'djunk'aga continued to treat He-nu Rabbit in this way, and she never retaliated.

Soon thereafter, another new girl, Weh-uh Turtle, started school. She was so beautiful Wak'djunk'aga went out of his way to be nice to her and impress her. Soon He-nu Rabbit and Weh-uh Turtle became friends. Besides being beautiful, Weh-uh also was kind and sweet, and she did not like the way Wak'djunk'aga treated He-nu.

Finally, Wak'djunk'aga could see how he had hurt He-nu Rabbit's feelings. He became a close friend to He-nu Rabbit. He had to learn the hard way to treat others as you would like to be treated.

Wak'djunk'aga's Quest for Food

By Ilona Maney, Bear Clan

One day, Trickster was wandering through the woods in search of food, and being awfully hungry he decided to camp. Sitting by his fire imagining what kind of food would taste good if he had some, he overheard two birds in a tree talking about a coyote with a magic trap and many caches of food, causing others to starve in nearby villages.

Trickster's hunger compelled him to devise a plan to steal the magic trap from the coyote, thus thinking he would never go hungry again. Trickster dug a very deep hole, camouflaging the opening with branches and leaves. He then went to visit Coyote and lied to him about seeing a family of fat squirrels and there were so many of them he needed help to catch them. Coyote told Trickster to show him the place where the squirrels lived and off they both went. Trickster told Coyote to creep toward a large bush and beyond that bush were all those fat squirrels. Coyote hastily crept toward the bush and fell into the trickster's hole, then Trickster buried Coyote alive. Trickster was so overjoyed that he happily jumped up and down, giving war whoops.

In the meantime, the birds informed the ones starving in the village about the caches of food and the magic trap and what Trickster had done to obtain all of it. The birds led a few villagers to the camp where the caches and the magic trap were located. Trickster caught the strangers at Coyote's camp and asked them why there were there. The villagers told Trickster they were having a large feast in the village and everyone near the village was invited. The villagers were to escort anyone they told of the feast back to the village right away and to waste no time doing so. Trickster thought to himself that it was good, because he could save the hidden caches of food for later, yet go elsewhere to eat food others had saved.

As they neared the village, the people escorting Trickster described in detail all the food that was to be offered at the feast, making Trickster drool at the mouth. He was more hungry than ever. As they entered the village, they told Trickster they made a wigwam for him to stay in while he feasted. So Trickster hurried over to his wigwam, to put his pack away, and upon entering promptly tripped over a stone. He fell, rolled into a very deep hole, and was buried alive.

Moral: Lying to obtain anything good in abundance and being greedy will only come back to haunt the liar.

Wak'djunk'aga
and the Car

By Dawn Makes Strong Move, Water Spirit Clan

One snowy day, Wak'djunk'aga was driving along a road as fast as he could. As he drove along, he came upon Brother Rabbit walking. He said to himself, "I bet Brother Rabbit is cold walking in the snow." So he stopped and picked up Brother Rabbit.

When Brother Rabbit got into the car, he immediately put on his seat belt after closing the door. "Thank you," said Brother Rabbit, "it sure is cold walking out in the wind and the blowing snow."

Once again Wak'djunk'aga started driving down the road as fast as he could. Not long thereafter, Wak'djunk'aga and Brother Rabbit met Brother Bear driving toward them. Brother Bear passed them and turned around; he then followed Wak'djunk'aga and Brother Rabbit. Wak'djunk'aga rolled down his window and called over to Brother Bear, who seemed to be pointing at the car, and asked, "Brother Bear, what seems to be the problem?"

Brother Bear answered, "Pull over to the side of the road. I want to talk to you."

"All right, Brother Bear," said Wak'djunk'aga. But he turned the wheel too sharply and slid off the road, down the ditch, up into a fence, and then crashed into a telephone pole.

Wak'djunk'aga went flying through the windshield and cracked his head open on the telephone pole. Wak'djunk'aga got up and held his head together with his hands. He turned and watched Brother Rabbit get out of the car and laughed at himself, and said, "It is for these things that people call me crazy."

Wak'djunk'aga
and the Car

Wak'djunk'aga
and the Ducks

By David Lee Smith, Thunder Clan

One spring evening, Wak'djunk'aga, the Winnebago trick-ster, was walking quietly along the forest trail. The only noise to be heard was the rumbling of his stomach, for Wak'djunk'aga had not eaten in days.

Then to the west of him, Trickster heard a drum beating. He left the trail and turned toward the beating of the drum. There was no trail there, so Wak'djunk'aga had to make his own path through the heavy underbrush. As he got closer to the noise he heard singing. Wak'djunk'aga thought to himself, "Whenever Indians sing, they always eat." So he formulated a plan in his mind as he grew nearer to the noise.

When Trickster reached the end of the underbrush, he parted the weeds and looked into the clearing. There was a long structure built there, and he knew it was a dance house. That is where the singing and the drumming were coming from. "So my friends are celebrating tonight," he said to himself. "That is good, because my stomach is getting louder with every step."

With very long strides, Wak'djunk'aga reached the dance house. He quietly pulled open the flap on the door and looked in. He was surprised at what he saw. There were hundreds of mosquitoes dancing around a large drum, where a large number of fireflies were beating on the drum with their wings. Then Wak'djunk'aga's stomach rumbled once more, saying in effect, "Hurry, find some food, I cannot take it anymore." With the noise of his stomach, the drummers and singers all turned toward Wak'djunk'aga, who was still peeking through the door.

The oldest mosquito said, "Look my brothers, it's Wak'djunk'aga our friend. Come, come help us sing and dance. We are celebrating the coming of spring." With that invitation, Wak'djunk'aga joined his friends in their merriment. After the next war dance, by looking through the hole in the top of the dance lodge the mosquitoes noticed that the stars were coming out. This hole is where the smoke escapes when the fires are lit.

The fireflies who were beating the drum with their wings then told Wak'djunk'aga that they must be on their way. Nighttime was approaching, and they and their mosquito brothers must be back on the job of lighting up the night and stinging people, as the Creator had willed them to do. With a rushing of their wings, all flew through the hole in the roof, and all were gone in the night, except Wak'djunk'aga and his hungry stomach.

Wak'djunk'aga with downcast eyes went out through the door into the moonlit night. He remarked to himself, "I should have eaten some of the mosquitoes. Now I have to go hungry another night." Then Wad'djunk'aga heard a familiar noise above him. It was the quacking of the ducks. Wak'djunk'aga knew that springtime was the season that ducks migrated back north from the south, where they spent the cold winter.

With that thought, an evil plan started working through Wak'djunk'aga's mind. He said to his stomach, "Now we will eat. We shall feast on the rich meat of roast duck." As if his stomach understood him, it stopped its rumblings.

Wak'djunk'aga quickly returned to the dance lodge and picked up the drum. With the drum stick, he started a song:

Come my brothers, let's celebrate the coming of spring.
Come my sisters, let's celebrate the coming of the little ones.

When the ducks passed over the dance lodge, they heard the song. The lead duck said, "Look my brothers and sisters, it's Wak'djunk'aga welcoming us back from our winter journey with a song." As they circled the lodge, another duck cried, "Let us go join our friend in dance and song, for we need a rest from our long journey." Even though he knew better, the lead duck relented, and all flew down to join their friend.

"Welcome, welcome," Wak'djunk'aga said. "I have been waiting for you for days." After drinking some water, he continued, "Here my friends, drink some cold water, and let us celebrate your journey north with a song."

When all the ducks had their fill, Wak'djunk'aga arranged them into a circle around the dance lodge. He started a slow war-dance song and then picked up the beat with a fast stomp-dance song. Now the ducks were really into it and they began dancing all over the place. Wak'djunk'aga now made his move and said, "Let us light the fires, for it will warm us and keep out evil spirits." After the fires were lit, the dancing continued.

When the third song was over, Wak'djunk'aga said, "My friends, before I start the fourth song you better close your eyes. It is getting pretty smoky in here and it will be bad for your eyes." The ducks closed their eyes, for they knew Wak'djunk'aga was right. They would need their eyes for the morning journey north. With that, Wak'djunk'aga picked up the beat, and with his other hand he picked up a war club that he had hidden.

Now the ducks were really into it, and they were all quacking to the beat of the drum. Whenever a duck got too near to the drum, Wak'djunk'aga hit the duck on the head and threw it over his head into a corner.

As the dance went on, the ducks started to pile up in the corner. By now, the lead duck knew something was the matter, because the quacking of the ducks was less intense than before. So he opened one eye, just in time to see Wak'djunk'aga hit one of his brothers and toss him into the corner, dead. With a loud quack, he screamed, "Escape! Escape, for Wak'djunk'aga is killing all of us!" All the ducks that were left opened their eyes and tried to escape through the hole in the roof. However, there was too much smoke in the room and their eyes began to turn red. After much confusion, the remaining ducks made their escape into the night with their now-red eyes. For that reason, all ducks today have red eyes, because of the smoke.

After his former friends were gone, Wak'djunk'aga carried all the dead ducks out of the dancing lodge and placed them by a fire. After cleaning them, he laid them row upon row over the hot coals. By now, it was after midnight, and Wak'djunk'aga knew that the ducks would not be ready until morning. With a rock as a pillow, he laid down to sleep, and counted roasted ducks in his dreams.

Wak'djunk'aga was not as crafty as he thought he was, for the craftiest creature that the Creator made was watching him through the tall weeds. This was Brother Fox. With a smile, Fox watched Wak'djunk'aga lie down to sleep and formulated his own plans for the roasted ducks.

When dawn was in the morning air, Brother Fox left his hiding place and made a beeline for the ducks. Since he had no bag to carry them away in, he sat there all through the early morning and consumed all the ducks and left Wak'djunk'aga all the bones. When all the roasted ducks were eaten, the sun lit the eastern horizon, and brother fox rolled off into the brush with his full stomach.

Wak'djunk'aga awoke with a smile. He was now ready for his feast. As he got up, he stared at the roasting pot with an open mouth, for all that was left was row upon row of duck bones. To this day, no one knows who made the loudest noise, Wak'djunk'aga or his hungry stomach. For being too greedy, he was denied his feast. Now he knew it is better to share than eat alone.

Turtle Trying
to Get Credit

A Tale

By Paul Radin

There was a village in which a chief lived. Turtle lived there, too.* The village was situated near a large river.

One day the Indians said to each other, "Look, the traders are coming." They were the Frenchmen. Finally the traders landed and settled in houses along the edge of the water down the stream. A large number of Indians immediately surrounded these houses. They were dressed in their best, with white and black wampum around their necks. Many of the women also wore earrings. The men were painted in various colors.

Everyone went there except Turtle. One day he said, "Younger brothers, the Indians are getting credit, and we also ought to be able to get some. However, I thought it would be better to wait till all the others are gone. They need clothing, and we do not need such things. ·If the others are able to get credit, I shall surely be able to do the same because all the traders are my friends." Thus he spoke to his younger brothers.

Story collected by David Lee Smith.

*The turtle, like the hare, belongs in the Trickster stories. They were all created by the Creator to help humans master life. The Winnebagos believed that there are four worlds in their cosmology, one beneath the other. After these supernatural beings helped humans master life and helped them on the right path, they went back to their own worlds. Maona is in charge of the heavens and he put Trickster in charge of the skies. Hare is in charge of the world. Turtle is in charge of the underworld.

Besides Turtle there were present Second-Born, the soft-shelled turtle, Third-Born, the snapping turtle (Keka), and Fourth-Born, the little red turtle. All these latter three were unmarried. Turtle himself, however, had a wife. He lived in a long lodge with two fireplaces. When he was ready to go, he said, "Now then, it is about time for us to go and get credit, for even these womanly fellows are getting it. Now I am going to talk to my friends."

When they got to the first trader, Turtle said to his companions, "This is my intimate friend, but let us go a little farther." When he came to another trader, he said the same thing, and thus they went from trader to trader until they came to the last man. There Turtle stopped and said, "Here we shall enter, for this man is a friend of mine."

As soon as they had entered, the trader came up to him and shook hands with him. "Second-Born (the soft-shell turtle), you try to get credit first." Then he asked the trader (for credit) but he was unsuccessful and so were the others.

"Turtle, I cannot do it," said the trader, "I was forbidden to do it when I started out. They told me that you are not to be trusted because you never repay what you borrow. They told me that you are lazy, that you don't even try to go out hunting, and that you gamble, and lie with women, and go on the warpath. Because you always do these things, I am forbidden to give you any credit. If you were to cheat me it would go hard with me because this is all the money I have. I cannot give you any credit. The other people have lots of money and perhaps they might help you out."

Then they went away and came to the trader nearest to this one. Turtle had said that this one never refused him, but when Second-Born went up to him and asked him for credit, the trader refused just as the other one had done. All four turtles pleaded with him a long time, but he absolutely refused. "Turtle," said this trader, "we are not going to buy any scalps." So again they failed. In like manner, Turtle went to all the traders, but they all refused.

"Younger brothers, you may all go home to your sister-in-law. I will return later as I want to finish some interpreting for which I was engaged, and besides, I want to have a good long talk with the traders." So the others went home and Turtle remained behind. There he stayed four days and nights without anything to eat. There were some young men drinking, but they always avoided him because they said that he would arrest them. All that was left for Turtle to do was to sleep at night near the campfires of the traders.

Turtle went around hungry, dusty, and his lips parched. The trader to whom he had gone first, seeing him in this plight, took pity on him and called him to his store and said, "Turtle, come here." Then he gave him some crackers, a can of fish, and a piece of cheese. "Turtle, when I looked at you this morning I took pity on you and I am going to give you a little credit. If you don't pay me I am willing to stand the consequences. This store is mine anyway. I know that giving you credit will be the same as throwing money away because you are noted for your worthlessness. That is the reason I was told to refuse you any credit. As soon as you get through eating, you may go after your wife and brothers and bring them here."

As soon as Turtle had finished eating, he went after his wife and his brothers. "Now then I have come after you. We are going to get credit. Those womanly fellows were the ones that had forbidden the traders to give me any credit, but now I have fixed it up. They told things that were not true about me, but that too I have fixed up. Now they are all after me so that I might ask them for credit, but I dislike them so we will go clear to the end of the road where we went the first time."

When they got to the end of the road, Turtle said, "Second-Born, you may go in first and get what you want." So Second-Born went in and bought the following things: a blanket and some yellow-edged broadcloth for leggings; some armlets and small buckles for his front hair braids; a pair of boots that reached up to his knees so that he could wear them when he went out wading to set traps or when he went hunting; some steel traps; and a gun. All these things he bought.

Then Turtle told the Third-Born to go in and get what he wanted. He bought the same things as the first one. As soon as Third-Born was through, Turtle sent Fourth-Born into the store. Fourth-Born bought the same things that his two elder brothers had bought, with the exception that he took a short gun instead of a long one.

"Aha!" said Turtle, when he saw his youngest brother coming out of the store with a short gun, "I always said that the youngest took most after me. All the others have bought guns entirely too long. With the gun you have bought, however, you can sit in a pit and load and thus you can fight."

"Say, Turtle," said the trader, "there you are at it again. That is why people speak so badly of you. You know that your brothers are not getting these guns for the warpath. But I knew that you were not a person to be trusted, and I knew that everything I trusted you with meant an absolute loss to me."

By this time, all Turtle's younger brothers had finished their trading. Then Turtle said to his wife, "Old woman, you may go in now and get whatever you think necessary, and after you have finished I will go in and get what I need." So the woman went in and bought kettles, dishes, knives, and some shot and powder. Then Turtle went in and got a small hand ax, four quarts of whiskey, and so on. When he was all finished, he told the trader that he was through and started home.

When he got home, he immediately began to gamble and continued doing so for many days. It was the fall of the year and some people had already left the village. Soon others went and before long only a very few were left. With these few, Turtle used to gamble. He lost everything, even the things that his younger brothers had bought for themselves. Soon everyone was gone and the turtles remained there alone. Then Turtle's younger brothers said, "I wonder why our elder brother is doing this. He ought to be out hustling for himself. I suppose he is going to stay here permanently. It is on account of these actions that the trader said those ugly things about him."

The next morning, Second-Born said, "Older brother, all the people have gone to the best hunting places. Why are we still here? Thus we were asking one another. So we decided that we should go somewhere." thus spoke the soft-shelled turtle.

"Oh my younger brother, you are right. That is what we also said last night, your sister-in-law and I. Long ago, when we were first married, we hunted in a place where there were many animals with furs. There we ought to go, we said. However, we were afraid that the other people might follow us, so we stayed here purposely so that we might go alone after the rest had left. It is not good to hunt with other people because they always rush forward in order to get ahead of you. So it is best to hunt alone and that is why I am doing this," Turtle said. "If they followed us and prevented us from hunting in the way we like best we would not be able to kill anything. So tomorrow we shall move." he said.

In the meantime, the traders were telling Turtle's creditor that Turtle was still around. "You see," they said to him, "what Turtle is doing, and that is why we were told not to give him any credit. All the things with which you trusted him he lost shortly after in gambling, as well as the things belonging to his younger brothers." Thus they spoke.

"I don't care. They were all my things and I did it because I took pity on him. I did it without expecting anything back." Thus spoke the trader.

Turtle moved very early the next morning and the soft-shelled turtle sat at the head of the canoe while Keka sat behind at the rudder. As soon as they had started, Turtle said, "Younger brother, Second-Born, as soon as we get to the place I will give you a warning because it is at a point where the creek empties into this water and is not noticeable. We will have to watch very closely for it is generally obstructed by young willows. As soon as one gets up the creek as far as that, the water becomes very deep. However, up a little ways farther it becomes a regular creek. When your sister-in law and I first got married I did my hunting here, and there used to be many furred animals, bear and deer. The creek was full of game in those days and the game must be even more abundant now for that was a long time ago. If they have been breeding ever since, there must be very many animals now." Thus he spoke.

The woman said the same thing. "Oh, when we were very young, your older brother hunted here. At that time he was not much more than a boy." Then Turtle spoke, "Now then, you must watch very closely as the place must be pretty near here. It is impossible to find it sometimes because often there are no signs of a creek. That is why they never hunt here. The water comes into it in a slightly different manner. That is the only way that one can tell whether one has reached it."

Then the soft-shelled turtle said, "Well, older brother, here is just such a place as you have described. Here the water seems to come in a sort of rushing way."

"This must be it, younger brother. Do not break any willows for if we are discovered the animals will be scared away from us in the hurry of other people to get as many animals as they can."

They cleared away the willows carefully as they went through, and they bent them back after they had passed. In this way there was no trace that anyone had passed through. After they had gone upstream a little way, sure enough the water became deeper. "Older brother, here the water is deeper," said the soft-shelled turtle.

"Yes, I told you that it used to be that way. It will get wider still as we go farther on, and finally it will become a chain of lakes. When we reach that place, we will strike our camp. In olden times it was a good camping place." Just as he had said, the creek began to get wider and soon they saw a beaver feeding on the shore. There were also otters there. "Older brother, I am going to shoot one."

Turtle, however, forbade him. "Don't do it, you will make them wild. Just leave them alone."

The game became more plentiful as they went along and the stream of water became wider. It was now evening.

"Second-Born," said Turtle, "shoot one of the larger ones so that we may eat it when we arrive. This shooting will not make them wild, especially if you draw your gun back immediately, for this will muffle the report. That is what I used to do when I wished to kill secretly."

So Second-Born shot one of the animals and sure enough the report of the gun was not very loud. Then they put the animal into the canoe, and Turtle said, "Second-Born, get out and walk. After a while you will come to the timber wood. Go toward it. That is where we used to live. It is a grove of red oak, and around the edge there used to be a growth of brush. Those you may use as frames for your furs. Have a fire ready."

At that place, therefore, he went ashore and they went on without him. Finally they heard the report of his gun. "Ah, he must have done that to a third-born (bear)," said Turtle. Finally they arrived at the place Turtle meant; they got out and walked. It was just as he had said. The timber wood was very thick and around the edge there was some brush. When they got to this place, they found the soft-shelled turtle building a fire already. He had a bear lying near him. Then immediately they built a lodge and the young men got ready to hunt.

Turtle then said to them, "Younger brothers, when the animals become wild it is impossible to kill many of them, so don't do it now. Besides the furs are not good yet. Come, help me camp so that your sister-in-law may make some soup for you." So then they all helped in the making of the lodge. They wanted to go hunting right away but he would not let them. They therefore, attended to the animals—the beavers and bears that they had already killed.

When they had finished their lodge, Turtle said, "My younger brothers, tomorrow morning we will get the materials for the frames on which we are to place the furs we obtain; go hunt, therefore, for the necessary wood." After a while, he continued and said, "Do not hunt (game) right away for the animals are likely to get wild if you hunt them too soon. Let us, therefore, settle down here for a while and not hunt until they get used to us, and then we will be able to kill them in great numbers. It is just because people kill them too soon that I dislike going hunting with them." Thus he spoke.

In the morning, they cut the frames for the furs, but the younger brothers said to one another, "We are tired of making these frames if we don't kill any game." Then Turtle said to them, "My younger brothers, you don't know anything about hunting if you are so desirous of hunting right away. Remember also, before letting your frames freeze, that you must dry them. That always makes the furs look better and permits the frames to be used over and over again. If the frames are not dried before they are allowed to get frozen they become very brittle." Turtle's younger brothers were very tired of making frames, however, and wanted to go hunting immediately.

Then Turtle spoke to them again and said, "My younger brothers, go out and get what we call a carry-all. This we generally make either of bark or simply of a piece of wood, and in that we can afterwards carry the furs that will be too heavy to carry on our backs." So they made a carry-all for themselves.

Thus they lived, only killing animals for food when their supply was exhausted. Turtle spoke to them again, "Younger brothers, as soon as it gets cold, let us make some racks for our furs. Otherwise the mice will gnaw holes in them." So they made some racks, intending to make more as soon as these were loaded with furs.

All winter they waited for the animals to get used to them and only shot animals when they needed them for food. The snow was now very deep, it was cold, and the waters were all frozen hard. "Well," said Turtle, "my younger brothers, let us begin to hunt. When the weather is like this, the animals don't pay much attention to themselves." The younger brothers dreaded to go out at that season, but he told them to get their carry-alls ready and start with him.

The first thing they came across was a beaver house. Turtle cut this open and went in and killed all the beavers who were there. Then he killed as many otters as he came across. It was very easy for there was no place to which they could run. His younger brothers were using their carry-alls to good purpose and brought home many animals. It was a very high pile of furs that they were able to stack up when they came home. At night Turtle and his wife would attend to the dressing of the skins. In the morning, when the young men were up, they saw all the furs hanging on the racks.

In this manner they continued, day after day, until their material for frames was exhausted. "Do you see now why I wanted you to make frames? But you paid no attention to me and got tired too soon. Now we shall have to hunt and get material for our frames at the same time. This is a nuisance." He tried to use the sticks that had been used before but they were all frozen and brittle, as the young men had not permitted them to dry first. However, he found a few that had been dried and these he could use again.

Then the furs were tied in bundles and placed on the racks and before long the racks were all covered. Finally they had gone over the entire hunting ground. The racks were overloaded so they roasted as much meat as they could. The young men continued hunting and were very successful. They killed many badgers and coyotes and skinned them and placed the furs on frames.

It was now spring and most of the people had returned to their summer village. Turtle, however, was nowhere to be seen. Everyone knew of everybody else's whereabouts; but of Turtle they knew nothing. "He must be killed," they said.

As they were hunting, Turtle said to his wife one day, "Old woman, I am going over to the village to see the people, for they must all be home by this time, and I will try to borrow my friend's boat if I can. Pack the worst furs for me." So they packed the coyote and badger skins for him and he started out. He got to the village at night.

"Ho ho! my friend. I have come back," he shouted.

"Ah, it is good," said his friend the trader, "for they were saying that you had been killed." Then the trader gave him some food.

When Turtle had finished his meal, he said to the trader, "My friend, I have brought over a few furs for you. They are just outside your door."

He went out, and sure enough there he found some furs. He thanked Turtle. "Really, my friend, it is good," he said. "I did not expect this, for I just wanted to get rid of the things and so I let you have them on credit. Indeed, it is good."

"My friend, I have only brought you the poorest furs I had. I have been hunting for you all winter, and I will bring you the others if you will let me have your boat. I will start early tomorrow morning and fetch you the other furs."

"It is good, but I will send my servants along with you, so you need not work. Now then, my friend, you must be tired, here therefore, is something for you to drink." Then he gave him four quarts of whiskey.

All night Turtle drank, and in the morning when the trader got up he gave him some more. Then he sent his servants along with many presents so that if Turtle was really telling the truth they could give them to him. Two servants went along and early in the morning they started. Turtle did not even have to do the rowing but instead drank all the time.

When they got to the creek, he told them it was over yonder. "The road will be full of broken sticks," he told them. After a while they got out of the boat and walked on foot. Turtle had to be led by the two servants because he was too drunk to walk. When they got there, the food was just cooking and the servants ate with the others. Then the servants carried the furs to the boat on long sticks that they had prepared.

They loaded on the boat all the furs that Turtle and his companions had obtained. Four days it took them to carry the furs to the boat, so many were piled up. Then when they were ready to start home, they put new clothes on Turtle: a black coat, what they called a king's coat, one with a red breast. Then they put a large quantity of wampum and four silver medals around his neck. They decorated him with armlets, bracelets, and yarn belts that they tied around his head. Finally they gave him four quarts of whiskey, and in this manner they came back. They wouldn't let him do the slightest bit of work and they treated him like a king.

About noon, the boat appeared some distance from the village. "Well," said the Indians, "it must be some trader's boat." But when they could see the occupants they recognized Turtle. "Why Turtle is in the boat," they said. He had the king's clothes on and he was drunk and was being held up by the servants. "Ho ho! It is Turtle. He has brought back very many furs," the Indians said, standing on the beach waiting for him. "Look, he has done a good season's work."

At the house of his friend, he brought his boat to the shore. The trader was very much surprised. Then the other traders said, "Turtle, let us buy some of the furs from you."

"They do not belong to me. They belong to my friend."

"Turtle, they are worth much more than all the stores here. Indeed they are worth a great deal more. Your friend hasn't got anything. He can't buy all those things."

"Nevertheless, I will not sell any of them to any of you because they belong to him, for it was for him that I hunted. I tried to get credit from you but you would not give me any, and you would not trust me. This man was the only one who would give me credit, so therefore, I determined to go out hunting for him and get him furs. They belong to him." He refused to talk to the others any more.

"My friend," said the trader to Turtle, "the entire store I give to you and I will go to my home in the morning as the boat is already loaded. The servants will watch the boat during the night as someone might want to steal something. All the whiskey in the store, too, belongs to you." The next morning the trader went home and Turtle remained in possession of the store.

Part Three

MYTHS OF THE
WINNEBAGOS

The
Ho-Chunk Boy
Who Fasted
Too Much

By David Lee Smith, Thunder Clan

Once long ago, when the Ho-Chunk people still lived among the pines, a big war developed between the animals and the people. In a village by a lake, the animals killed everyone except a small boy and his grandfather. When the young boy reached seven years of age, the grandfather spoke to him. "My son, you and I are the only people left in this village. If there is anything you want, you must ask the spirits for help. But always remember, you have to fast before you pray."

So the young boy fasted and fasted. One day, the grandfather talked to his grandson, "My grandson, surely the spirits have answered your prayers by now, because it is not good to fast for too long."

The boy replied, "They did answer my prayers, Grandfather. They made me a great hunter; they made me a great medicine man. I can cure anything." The boy continued, "I cured the dog of insects. I cured the birds of the sky."

When the grandfather left, the boy continued to fast. This made the grandfather very worried. So he approached his grandson a second time. He spoke, "My grandson, it was not meant that humans should fast too long. Surely you have received more powers from the spirits. Why do you continue to fast?"

The boy replied, "Grandfather, I want to live forever. I never want to die." The grandfather left his grandson with a sorrowful look on his face, and the young boy continued to fast.

One night, Ma-ona the Creator called the spirit beings together and debated on what to do with the little boy. It was decided to grant the young boy his wish. The next morning the grandfather went to wake his grandson, but found him dead.

The grandfather was heartbroken. He then prepared the young boy's body for burial. For four days he had a wake. All the boy's friends came, as did some animals. After the morning of the fourth day, the grandfather buried his grandson.

On the anniversary of the young boy's death, the grandfather put on a feast for his departed grandson's friends. This was the traditional way. When the feast was over, he approached the grave of his grandson with an offering of food. To his surprise, there was a tree growing there. For the next three years, after each feast, the tree grew bigger and bigger.

Finally, the grandfather knew the meaning of the tree. His grandson got his wish after all. Ma-ona the Creator made his grandson into a tree, because trees tend to live longer than humans. So the grandfather was happy. So ends the story of the little boy who fasted too much.

The Story of
Watequka
and His Brothers

Author unknown

Once upon a time there was a long lodge in which dwelt
several brothers. They went hunting every day, but left the
youngest one at home. The eldest brother said to the ones
who went hunting, "You are my brothers. Hunt just as you
deem best." In the morning they all departed, leaving the
youngest one to take care of the lodge.

By and by, a man entered the lodge very suddenly, saying
to the youth, "Whither have your brothers gone?"

The youth replied, "They have all gone hunting."

"I have come to invite your brothers to play a game;
therefore, when they come home in the evening be sure to
tell them." The youth consented, but when his brothers
returned, he forgot about the man who had come in the
morning.

The next day, the brothers departed again. Again did the
stranger appear, repeating his request. Once more did the
youth forget to tell his brothers. After a like experience on
the third day, the visitor threatened the youth with trouble
if he failed to deliver his message. When he learned on the
fourth morning of the youth's negligence, he became very
angry, knocked him down, and beat him severely.

After the departure of the man, the youth took a stick and
hit it upon the ground while saying, "I will tell my brothers

Story collected by David Lee Smith from the
Anthropological Archives, Smithsonian Institution.

when they come home." He continued saying this all day. When evening came, the eldest brother returned and was alarmed at beholding the strange behavior of his youngest brother. He was at a loss how to proceed. At length he said, "Oh my brother, what is the matter with you?"

But the youth spoke not. He continued doing as he had done during the day. At length all the brothers returned. Then the youth told them about the invitation brought by the man. Then the eldest brother said, "Let us go tomorrow." In the morning the eldest brother led them. When they had reached the top of a hill, they found a lodge there in which men were awaiting them.

The eldest brother spoke to the men inquiring the nature of the contest. The men on the other side said that they would contend in a race. After agreeing to this, the eldest brother urged his brothers to tell about their dreams or visions. The youngest brother said that he had a vision of the sun. So it was decided that the youngest brother should contend against the other men. Bets were made, and the opponents proceeded to the starting point. They said that they would run back after reaching a large prairie. On noticing that the youth dropped a little behind in the race, the eldest brother exclaimed, "Oh youngest brother, why are you lagging behind?"

Then the youngest brother started to run a little faster. His opponents had almost reached the goal, when the youth made a desperate effort and distanced them all. He seized the banner and carried it off to the great delight of his brothers. They gave shouts of triumph. The victors took the stakes and carried them home.

The next day, they went hunting again. In their absence the man who had previously come to invite them entered the lodge again. He spoke to the youngest brother and said that his people wished to engage in another contest. The youth informed him that his brothers would be told, and on their return in the evening he delivered the message. The eldest brother said that they would accept the invitation. They started in the morning, and on their arrival found their opponents waiting for them.

After betting, it was decided that there should be a wrestling match. The eldest brother said that he would wrestle with them. The contest lasted throughout the day. Late in the evening, the eldest brother threw his opponent to the ground. He and his brothers seized the stakes and started home.

The next day, they all remained at home. The man entered the lodge suddenly, as on previous occasions, and invited them to another contest. They said that they would go. In this manner they went thither regularly every other day.

A
Winnebago
Myth

By W. C. McKern

Old-Woman lived on the land with her grandson. Young-Man wore nothing but a feather in his hair. One day, Old-Woman was picking herbs. "A man cannot kill animals without a bow and arrows," she said.

Young-Man said, "How could I know that? You who know should have told me of this. While wandering about I saw all kinds of animals."

"Yes, I should have told you about it," Old-Woman said. "You are right about that," she said. "That will be a hard proposition. I shall make a bow and arrows for you. Go upon the bluff and cut hickory."

When he returned from the bluff, he carried basswood. Finally he brought some hickory. Old-Woman made a bow. When it was prepared and dried, she hung it up.

"Now get some gray bark dogwood," she said.

"Yes, I am familiar with that," he said, but he brought back poplar. After a second trip, he brought back dogwood. Then she said, "I said it would be a hard proposition."

"Grandmother, lend me your elk-horn club," he said. So she let him have it. He went hunting in the early morning. Then he saw a big buck. He waited in hiding. Then he chased it and killed it. He carried home the entire deer by means of his pack-strap. Old-Woman laughed at her grandson for doing this. Then she showed him how to carry a deer.

Story collected by David Lee Smith.

The old lady was surprised at his prowess. She said, "This meat is good to eat." It was the first deer meat they had eaten.

"You should have told me to do that long ago," he said.

Then she spoke to him again. "It is going to be a hard proposition; the arrows must be feathered. Go hunt for turkey." Again he borrowed her club. He hunted for turkey. He killed two of them to obtain feathers for the arrows. Old-Woman thanked him. "This is another kind of meat that is good to eat," she said. The meat was cooked. The skin she blew up with air and hung to dry in the house.

Old-Woman said to him, "It is going to be a hard proposition. We will need glue from the body of the sturgeon to glue the feathers on the arrows."

"Where can I find some?" Young-Man asked.

"Go down to the river; there you will find some."

So he went there. Old-Woman had an awl. This he borrowed. In the morning, he cut a hole in the ice. There he waited. Of one he asked, "Is Sturgeon what they call you?"

"They call me Pickerel," that one said. "Sturgeon stays in the middle of the river, in the deep places."

After that, he went to a place where the water was deep and waited there. He inquired of another and that one said that he was Sturgeon. "Are there more of you there?" he asked.

"No, but there are others following me," said that one. So he killed two of them. Then he went home. Old-Woman was pleased.

"This is another kind of good meat," she said. From it she prepared glue for him. Then she fixed feathers on the arrows. But there were no arrowheads. This Young-Man noticed and wondered what next was to be done. Old-Woman filled a sack with acorns and placed it on her back. Then she carried it to a certain man. There she exchanged the acorns for arrowheads and departed. Old-Woman returned home with the arrowheads and fixed them to the arrows. But there was no quiver. He had to carry the arrows in his hand.

He hunted in the early morning. "With these," he thought, "I shall kill all kinds of animals." Then he knew that there were deer approaching. So he fitted an arrow to his bow and told it to go. The arrow did not move. All day long he continued to do this. He did not see how he could kill a deer this way. He placed the arrow in the fork of a tree and told it to go, but it would not. He gave up in disgust and threw his bow and arrows away.

At evening, when he returned home, he complained, "I could not kill anything with those arrows."

Old-Woman said, "Why, they used to kill all kinds of animals with them."

"Then how do you work it? Tell me that!"

So she told him how. Thus she shot at the turkey skins that were hung to dry. "That is the way to shoot," she said. He tried it. He learned how it was done. "That's right!" she said. He could hardly sleep that night.

Then, the very first thing in the morning, he went. He brought back deer on his back. Again he hunted. Four times he returned with a deer. At last he knew how to kill deer. Then he made a quiver of deer skin. After that he hunted for nothing but deer. Old-Woman ceased to gather herbs and vegetables.

Sometime after that, Old-Woman went to the bluff. She returned with hickory sticks that she split and made into lacrosse sticks. Her grandson returned home and asked her what they were for. "This is called lacrosse," she said. "When they gamble they use this." So he did not hunt anymore. Here was something new. Next morning, Old-Woman made for him a ball, and showed him its use. Old-Woman understood the game, but Young-Man could not get it straight. Finally he learned how it went. Then Old-Woman ceased her instructions, but he practiced the game all the time.

Sometime later he said, "Grandmother, tomorrow I shall practice all alone. You must not watch me." So next morning he went to the open prairies. There followed a great uproar, as from many people.

Old-Woman wondered. "What people can have come? He didn't tell me about this," she thought. She was anxious to investigate and see what it was all about, but he had forbidden her to look, so she didn't go. Old-Woman contemplated spying, just a glimpse, she thought. He wouldn't know anything about it. When she peeked out, her grandson was approaching all alone. Arriving home, he took his bow and arrows with him and went out again. Toward evening he brought back a deer.

Old-Woman said, "Grandson, I interfered with you in your game."

"Yes," he said.

Next morning, he went out again to play. Again she heard it. A great uproar, she heard. Again she thought she would like to investigate the source of the commotion. She peeked outside as before. She saw no one. Old-Woman heard the whistle of eagle feathers on his head. A third time Old-Woman interfered with his playing in this way.

Then while he prepared to play a fourth time, he said, "You have spied too much. You might cause me to be defeated." As the time to start the game neared, there came a snowstorm. Great snowflakes fell.

The Old-Woman said, "They are challenging you. If you accept, then you must tie me up before leaving."

After that, he played the crowd all day long. Old-Woman tried to untie herself. She could not get loose. In the evening, there was shouting. "We won," someone said. Young-Man came in through the door wet with perspiration.

"Oh, my grandson, did you win?" she asked.

"Yes," he said. Then he untied her. So at evening they ate together. After that, he played no more. From that time on he began to spend his time hunting.

Old-Woman said, "Grandson, you should practice acting like a son-in-law." Then he said "Grandmother, how is that done?"

Then Old-Woman said, "They used to drive a whole drove of elk right up to the village and kill them right there. They would only take the tongues." That is how he did it.

He left in the morning. A whole drove of elk he rounded up and killed all of them. At this time he felt spirit power within himself. He shot a single arrow and killed a multitude. So he returned home with only the tongues on his back.

Old-Woman was glad. "Aha! You have done well. Someday you surely must take a woman," she said. "At last it is time for you to have a woman," she said.

"But I do not know where a woman is to be found," he said. "There are no people near us, Grandmother. Whence is she to be obtained, for there are no people anywhere about us."

"You are wrong," Old-Woman said, "There are plenty."

In the morning, he got ready. "You do not look good in that bearskin blanket," she said. So she dressed him differently. Three times she arranged his dress. The fourth time she covered him with a white blanket and put red leggings on him. About his neck she placed wampum and a gorget.* In his hand was a stone pipe. Finally, she gave him a fishskin tobacco pouch. He filled this with a mixture of tobacco and kinikinik.

Then Old-Woman told him to travel toward the east. She said, "You will come to a big prairie with a big bluff standing in the center. When you enter this prairie, run fast. You consider yourself swift of foot. Run as fast as you can. Hasten at top speed and climb the bluff. Then you must shout, *Korotc'* [I win]. Someone will say it after you. He will say it just as you say it. When you look around you will see a naked fellow who wears nothing but moccasins and carries only a bow and arrows. You will not be able to get rid of him. He will never let you escape. Somewhere you will stay overnight with him. When you stop to sleep, he will urge you to tell a story. If you do not tell a story, he will tell you all about what we are now doing here. He will tell all about us. In the evening he will tell this to you. He will help you. He will be your friend." So Old-Woman spoke.

---

*Wampum is a string of small, painted shell beads. A gorget is a medallion.

So in the morning he departed toward the east. Soon he came upon an open prairie. Then he started to run. He increased his speed as he approached the bluff and climbed to its top. Then he shouted, "*Korotc.*" Then behind him, Naked-One also shouted, "*Korotc.*" "Listen," he said, "I am first; I said it before you did." Then they argued. Afterwards they sat and smoked. That one smoked black ash, but Young-Man smoked a mixture of tobacco and kinikinik. Naked-One smelled it and quit smoking. Young-Man sat watching his face. Then he gave some to him and said to him, "I said *Korotc* first, so I give you some tobacco."

Next morning they started out again on their journey. Then Naked-One said, "I must repair a moccasin string; wait for me." But Young-Man didn't wait. He remembered what his grandmother had told him about escaping. This fellow was altogether too smart. So he selected one of his arrows and shot it. It fell where a pine tree stood far away. He spoke and it was so; like his arrow, he fell far away in the midst of some thick brush and vanished, just as he had wished. Late in the afternoon he came to a big log and hid there.

That other one did the same thing. He came to the hiding place of Young-Man and said, "Say it was I who said '*Korotc*' first. Why are you hiding?"

Young-Man said, "I am not hiding; it is a custom among my people to do this way."

Then they built a fire. There they slept. Naked-One went out into the outer darkness and returned with a bear. He just kicked a small mound and out of it came a bear. Old-Woman's grandson pulled out the arrow. Naked-One forbade him, but he pulled it out. Naked-One told him not to touch the bear, but he touched it. So Naked-One gave the bear to him. He accepted it, and said, "You have given me spirit power, I said '*Korotc*' first and so you have favored me."

He singed the hair off the bear. Then he began to handle it. It became very small, just like a red squirrel. Then he cooked it. He made a pile of wood sticks for it. Then he cut the bear into pieces and placed them there. When he had finished, the size of the parts of the bear was all restored again. Naked-One stuck an arrow up beside the fire, and said, "You must eat this whole bear. If you do not finish it all I will shoot you with this arrow." Young-Man was pleased. Then he began to eat. He ate steadily until all was eaten. Naked-one smiled, surprised.

Young-Man said, "I said *'Korotc'* first. All by myself I ate it all. If you don't eat it will look bad. I will hunt something for you." So he, too, kicked a little mound, and when the bear came out he killed it. In the same way he forbade Naked-One to take out the arrow, or to touch the bear, but Naked-One did not obey him. "Oh well, you can have it then," said Young-Man, "I forbade you, but you took it anyway."

Naked-One said, "You have given me spirit power." Then he in turn did that; he handled the bear and it became as small as a red squirrel. He singed off its hair, then he cooked it and cut it into pieces. These he placed upon the pile of sticks.

Young-Man stuck up arrows beside the fire, and said, "If you leave as much as a mouthful unfinished, I will shoot you with these."

"All right," said Naked-One. He ate it all. So they were both even. Then they filled their pipes and began smoking together. Naked-One said, "Why don't you tell some stories?"

Young-Man said, "How is that? I said *Korotc* first; I was the first one."

"Say, you are right," said Naked-One, "I was the first to say *Korotc*, so I will begin telling stories. This is my story:

"Once Old-Woman and her grandson were living together. The Old-Woman used to advise him. She taught him how to run swiftly. The grandson thought he was a fast runner. Then she made a bow and arrows for him. She told him how to hunt. She told him how to practice being a son-in-law. So he did as he was told. The time came when he was expected to marry. He sought a village. He was well dressed. Before he departed, she said to him, 'Grandson, I will tell you something.' Old-Woman thought she possessed spirit power. Young-Man thought too she possessed this power. Young-Man also thought that he was equally powerful. So she said to him, 'When you come to a prairie, start running. Run with all your might.' She said to him, 'At the foot of the bluff run even faster and climb the bluff at top speed. When you reach the top say *Korotc*. Then you will see a naked man back of you. He, too, will say *Korotc*.' But Old-Woman's grandson was beaten there. Sure thing! He was entirely outrun. Then the naked man said, 'Wait for me unit I fix my moccasin string.' But as soon as he was out of sight, Young-Man shot an arrow that fell in a thicket of pine scrub, and like the arrow, he fell there, too. The naked man did the same thing in just the same way. There he found the young man lying in hiding. The naked man said, 'Hey, there! I said *Korotc* first. Where are you?' Young-Man stood up and answered, 'Hey there! I am the one who said *Korotc* first. This hiding business is just a custom of my people.' Then they built a fire. There they were; ha! It was right where we are now." That is what he said.

"Well!" said Young-Man. "Is that all the story you have to tell?"

"Remember," said Naked-One, "it was I who said *Korotc* first. Now it is your turn to tell a story."

"Sure, I can tell stories," said Young-Man.

"A man who had ten brothers became angry and ran away from his folks. Entirely naked he went away from his home. His brothers wondered what he would do but they did not try to stop him. Then this fellow thought, 'Why did I do such a thing?' He was ashamed of himself. 'Alas!' he said, for he was afraid to go back. Naked he wandered about. Through the wilderness he roamed with no habitation in which to live. Now a certain fast runner went courting. The naked man watched him. 'Well!' said he, 'Men who go courting certainly wear fine clothes!' Then he schemed how he could get some of the clothing. He waited for the young man at the bluff. He planned to win some of the garments by climbing to the top of the bluff first. But ho! The other outran him. So that's my story," said Young-Man.

"Ho!" thought Naked-One. "Somehow or other I must get some of them." He would steal them while Young-Man slept, he thought. But Young-Man kept awake all night. At daybreak, Naked-One, lying close to the fire, fell asleep. "Ah!" said Young-Man. When daylight came, he saw that the fellow was asleep. Then Young-Man took off all his clothing. Only his bow and arrows he retained. Then he ran away. Before he was out of sight, Naked-One awoke, and shouted to him, "I said *Korotc* first!" "Why are you leaving me?" No answer.

Young-Man found some clothes there ahead of him. Then he sat down and put them on. Then Naked-One was there, saying, "I said *Korotc* first. Why did you leave these clothes with me?"

Young-Man answered, "Why did you not put these on? Ha! You are no animal. I am not going to lead you naked to my destination where I go to seek a wife."

"Oh, it is good," said Naked-One. "My friend, I am pleased. Sometime, if there is need of it, I will die for you. But just the same, I said *Korotc* first. That is why you gave me these clothes."

Then he put on the clothes. They looked almost exactly like each other. The bows and arrows were different; the arrows of Naked-One had no feathers, and his bow had one serrated edge.

So they started their journey. They approached a village. They came to its outskirts about noon. There lived an old woman with her grandson, a youth approaching manhood. When they arrived, she placed a new mat and a bearskin for them to sit on and called them grandsons. While they were seated, she said to them, "You have come after the chief's daughters." They both laughed.

"Oh, no." They flatly denied it.

But the old woman said, "Oh, do not deny it; that is what you came for. They are out there carrying wood for me."

Then she put the pot on to boil, just a few beans in a very small pot. It looked like but two mouthfuls, they thought. They would have to go hungry, they thought. When it was cooked, she put some in a wooden bowl and left it to cool. Then she gave it to them. Then they began to eat. But they could not eat it all. They did their best but they were absolutely stuffed. Finally they gave up. So they both had to say, "We pass it on to our friend here."

The old woman smiled and said, "My grandsons, you both thought that there was not enough. Why did you not eat it all?" So the old woman's grandson put it all in his mouth at one time with a wooden spoon and turned the bowl bottom side up.

Again she said to them, "You have come after the chief's daughters. I am glad of that." In a little while, the chief's daughters came in carrying wood on their backs. There were three of them: First-Born, Second-Born, and Third-Born.

First-Born brought her wood into the house. "Oh!" she exclaimed, and hastened out. Then she told the others. So Second-Born brought in her wood. Finally, Third-Born entered the house. She closely observed the strange men. She noted their manner of dress. The only difference was in their bows and arrows, and Naked-One had a snakeskin head-band. Each wore in his hair a large middle feather from an eagle's tail.

She remembered every detail of each costume. The other girls asked her about it, but she refused to tell them. "The idea! You saw them before I did," she said. Then they returned to their homes, where men were playing the moccasin game. They were betting wampum.

Mud-Turtle was there. He was gambling with the others. Nearby the girls talked together. Mud-Turtle heard all that they said. He then knew what was going on. The girls had seen someone. He saw Third-Born whispering about it to her father. The father spoke loudly so that the others could not hear what she said. She told all that she had seen to her father.

Then Mud-Turtle spoke, "It must be late in the afternoon." The others said, "You are just making an excuse so that you can quit the game."

He answered, "Oh, I don't care about that, but some friends of mine are coming. I expected them yesterday."

They smiled, "You just want to quit, that's all. No one is coming here."

He said, "It is customary to discourse on some matter and to talk until it is late. That is why they have not yet arrived. They should be here by this time, I should think."

Then the chief said, "Whenever people come here you call them your friends. That's the way you do."

"I speak the truth," said Mud-Turtle. "When one was with his grandmother, she dressed him in a very fine suit." They asked Mud-Turtle what kind of suit it was. "Ha!" he said, "It was a white blanket for the body, red leggings to put on, a necklace of wampum, a gorget, and eagle-tail feather in the hair, paint for the face, and a fishskin pouch full of mixed tobacco and kinikinik; that is how they will be dressed," he said. "One has arrows without feathers and a bow notched on one side and his headband is of snakeskin."

The chief then said, "Your friends are the ones." Then he turned the wampum over to Mud-Turtle and pushed it toward him. "These are your women; take them back," he said.

Mud-Turtle instructed his wife to boil dried beaver meat and sweet corn for his friends. Then he went to the old woman's house after them. But others were there ahead of him to see the strangers and offer them food. The strangers knew of his approach by the sound of his rattles. They asked, "Grandmother, who comes?" She answered, "Mud-Turtle, it is he." They smiled.

When he came into the house he walked right in. He greeted the strangers. "Well, here you are," he said. "Good. I expected you yesterday. Perhaps you were delayed." Both of them smiled.

"You are right," they said, "That is how it happened."

Then they went home with Mud-Turtle. He invited them to eat. He supplied them liberally with wampum.

"My friends, you must stay with us for a long while," he said. In the evening he took them back to the old woman's house.

Then he conducted them to the house of the chief. When they arrived there, Mud-Turtle went in alone. He told the daughters that the strangers had come to that place after them. "They much desire to come in and see you," he said. To this the girls agreed. Mud-Turtle told the strangers. After that they returned to the old woman's house. There they remained for the night.

In the morning, another came and invited the strangers to come and eat. Mud-Turtle went along with them. The man was named Curly-Haired-One; the woman was called Long-Hair. "These are our friends," said Mud-Turtle, "so you may stay here over night if you care to." Then Curly-Haired-One presented them with wampum. "This is what we gamble with," he said. "You can join in a game if you wish."

To still another place Mud-Turtle and his new friends were invited. When they arrived there, they saw that the house was like the other had been, covered with elk hide. That one said, "Come over whenever you feel like it." He then served mashed corn with wild rice. It was the first time in their lives that the strangers had tasted this food. It was delicious.

Then Mud-Turtle said, "This is another of our friends."

Trickster replied, "Yes, these are all my friends." Then he, too, gave the strangers wampum. Then they departed. Mud-Turtle stayed right with them.*

That night, Naked-One visited the house of the chief. He told his friend that he would marry First-Born. When he returned, Young-Man said, "I have made a plan. Let the grandson of the old woman of the house sleep between us tonight." So they placed the grandson there.

In the morning, Young-Man made for him a suit. Like their own suits it was made; a white blanket, red leggings and fishskin tobacco pouch. Next morning the old woman could not find her grandson. She became quite angry for he

---

*Trickster is sometimes involved in affairs with supernatural beings, but he spends most of his time with humans to teach them to walk the right path of life. See W. C. McKern, "A Winnebago Myth," Public Museum of the City of Mulwaukee *Yearbook* 9 (1929): 215-30.

was not opposite the door where he was accustomed to lie. Finally she went out after water. Then the three young men got up. Soon the old woman returned. "Grandmother," they called, "can you tell us apart? Which is he who stays with you?"

Then she studied them. "It is you," she said to Young-Man. "No, it is you," she said to Naked-One. But they showed her that they had placed her grandson in the middle. Then she was pleased. Thus they planned to marry the girls; the old woman's grandson should marry Third-Born. That night they all were married.

Next morning all were sleeping. The old woman awakened them. She said to them, "Sons-in-law should go hunting."

"This is how we will do it," they answered. "Borrow arrows for us from the chief's household."

When she came to the chief's house, they asked her what she wanted. "My grandsons have taken wives; they wish to go hunting." So she collected arrows and brought them home.

Mud-Turtle went along with the hunters. Then they stopped and made plans. They considered hunting methods. Young-Man spoke, "Let us round up a drove of elk," he said to them. Naked-One and the old woman's grandson decided to kill bears. Naked-One kicked a hill and bears came out. Then they killed them. The old woman's grandson shot into a blackened stump and a bear fell out on the ground, dead. Mud-Turtle said he would go back to the village to get someone to come and carry the bears home. After that, ten bears were killed.

Mud-Turtle arrived at the chief's house. "My friends have taken wives and are hunting," said Mud-Turtle. "If I was still young, I would have gotten here long ago. But now I am old. Some are needed to carry in the game. They should start out at once." A crier was instructed. The head of every household was notified. All day long they worked at it.

Young-Man returned home late in the evening. He brought a drove of elk with him. Then he killed them all.

Only the tongues he took. Young-Man said, "Grandmother, take these home on your back." The old woman could not carry them. Young-Man said, "Tell them that the elk are just over the hills. Go after them in the morning." Then he drove up a herd of deer and killed them all.

Mud-Turtle said, "So you have come here to live. I am glad of that."

"So am I," said Young-Man.

"I will help you out," said Mud-Turtle. Then he brought moss from the river and threw it on the bank. It was changed to beavers. There were many sizes, large and small. Then they carried them all into the village. After that they stopped hunting. There was an abundance of meat.

Then Young-Man left the house of the old woman and moved into the village, to the house of the chief.

At that time, gambling games were started. Then all the people were crying. "We shall all be killed," they said. "The man-eating giants have come." That is why they were afraid.

Mud-Turtle said, "Ha! Have no fear. Even if I was all alone, I could do almost anything. But now my friends are here with us."

The chief said, "In this matter I have no voice; everything is turned over to you and your friends. You are indeed brave men."

A giant came and asked for the chief, but it was Mud-Turtle who directed him across the prairie. "Camp there in the open prairie," he said. "There we can play lacrosse."

Then the giant returned to his people. Said he, "A certain man directed me to camp across the open prairie, but I do not think he is the chief. He said we could thus have a good place in which to play lacrosse."

"Ha! Mud-Turtle! That's the fellow," said the others. "Of course he had to be there. He is a crafty fellow to play against." So they said.

At the chief's house, the people were gathered together. Mud-Turtle said, "We shall listen to what those fellows are saying." He spread out wood ashes on the ground. Then he held his head down to listen. He heard them talking. "They say that they will have lacrosse sticks ready for use in the morning," he said.

Next morning, the giants came. Then they said, "Let us play lacrosse."

"That is good," said Mud-turtle. "We have some goods here to wager."

"That is good," said the giants. "But my people have nothing here to wager."

So the Indians held a meeting at the chief's house. Curly-Haired-One was invited, and Trickster, too. Meat and tobacco were served. Then Mud-Turtle explained who the giants were, and their sons-in-law who came with them. These were Red-Fox, Red-Tailed-Hawk, Fisher, Pretty-Woman-with-Red-Hair (a very fast runner), and Rough-Legged-Hawk.

Then they decided to play Curly-Haired-One against Red-Fox, Naked-One against Red-Tailed-Hawk, Trickster against Fisher, Young-Man against Pretty-Woman-with-Red-Hair, and the old woman's grandson against Rough-Legged-Hawk. Then Mud-Turtle spoke, "Trickster, be sure not to do anything foolish, whatever you do."

In the morning they went toward the prairies. They hung garments on a pole. The giants, however, knew what they had come after. There was no question about that. The giants said, "We will wager men."

Mud-Turtle answered, "If we had known that we were to kill each other, we would have come over to your place early in the morning and killed you all off." So they decided to wager men. Mud-Turtle wagered half of the inhabitants of the village.

The giants had a redstone ball. "Ha!" said Mud-Turtle. "We cannot use that very well; someone might be hit with it and so be killed." So they did not use it. A ball was thrown up and the game was on. Red-Fox got the ball, but Curly-Haired-One chased him; finally he caught him. He split Red-Fox nearly half in two. The giants complained about this killing of Red-Fox.

Curly-Haired-One picked up Red-Fox and threw him to one side. Then he said to him, "Many people have suffered at the hands of certain ones with whom you have banded yourself. From now on be satisfied to depend upon mice for your sustenance." Then Red-Fox ran away from there and was seen no more. Then Curly-Haired-One said, "Your son-in-law has gone away to hunt mice."

The game was resumed. Red-Tailed-Hawk ran away with the ball this time, but Naked-One knocked him down with his lacrosse stick. Naked-One picked him up and threw him to one side. "You shall subsist upon snakes from now on," he said to Red-Tailed-Hawk, "Earth-Maker did not create you to bring affliction to humans. You do not belong with these giants."

Then Rough-Legged-Hawk ran away with the ball. In the same way, the old woman's grandson caught up with him and struck him down. Then he picked him up and threw him to one side. "Hereafter," he said to him, "you shall live on mice alone. With these giants you have brought evil to humans. Earth-Maker did not create you for this purpose." Rough-Legged-Hawk ran away and was seen no more.

Next Fisher—part bear, part fish—got the ball and ran. Trickster finally caught him. With his lacrosse stick he chased Fisher up a tree. Then he struck him down and killed him. He picked him up and threw him to one side. "From now on," he said to the immortal Fisher, "you will eat nothing but the honey you find." So Fisher ran away and was seen no more.

Then Pretty-Woman-with-Red-Hair took the ball, but Young-Man took the ball from her and ran with it. Young-Man wore earbobs, of human head, which he now uncovered. Pretty-Woman-with-Red-Hair caught up with him. She saw the earbobs. They were smiling at her. She became embarrassed. They stuck out their tongues at her. They winked at her. The giants were also embarrassed. They laughed until it nearly killed them. That is when they named this Young-Man He-Whose-Earbobs-Are-Human-Heads.

So they won the game. Mud-Turtle killed all the wagered giants. When the game was over, the Indians gathered at the chief's house. When evening came they ate. They did not kill Pretty-Woman-with-Red-Hair. They brought her home alive.

Mud-Turtle prepared again to listen to the giants. They were saying, "If we had used our own ball, we would have won."

In the morning, the giants came and demanded another game. Mud-Turtle refused to play. The giants then said, "The losers make this request; whatever the losers ask cannot be denied." So the challenge was accepted.

The redstone ball was used. Once, as if by accident, the giants threw the ball among the Indian spectators and killed many of them. But the people made no complaint. So they scored over them. Another time, as if by accident, Mud-Turtle threw the ball among the giant spectators, and killed many in the same way.

Then a giant threw the ball at Mud-Turtle, but he was wearing a rawhide shield that protected him. The ball bounced away from him toward the giants and killed many more of them. Mud-Turtle said, "That is fine! Do that some more."

So they won again. After they had killed all the wagered giants, they covered them with cattail down and burned them. The giants said to them, "We will dance tonight; in the morning we will play again some game or other." Then they departed.

All the people gathered at the chief's house. When evening came they ate. Mud-Turtle said, "Again I will listen to them. What is this they are saying?" He smiled. After leaving the playing field, all the young people of the giants had run away. When the water drum sounded, only the old ones were left to participate in the dance.

So in the morning, the Indians went in pursuit. There were Mud-turtle and his friends, four of them all told. When they arrived at the camp of the giants, they killed the drummer first. Then they pursued the others. Soon they came to a place where the path forked. They followed one branch and caught up with some of them. They killed all of these.

Turning back, they followed the other branch to the edge of the ocean. There they caught up with the rest of the giants. They killed all of them. Only a youth and a girl of the giants were left. These two they spared. To them the four Indians said, "Never again abuse two-legged people with whom you are walking."

They returned to the village. Everybody was happy over what had been accomplished.

Then a son was born to Young-Man. The chief said, "My daughters, my sons-in-law must have homes of their own from which they have come. Their people in their own country will be worrying about them." Then the two friends, Young-Man and Naked-One, took their wives with them to their homes. Young-Man also took Pretty-Woman-with-Red-Hair with him. They stopped where they previously had camped on the way there. Next morning, Naked-One said, "My friend, here will I make my home." Young-Man journeyed on to the home of his grandmother.

When they arrived, Old-Woman saw the baby and was proud of it. Old-woman greatly admired Pretty-Woman-with-Red-Hair.

Then Young-Man went hunting and brought home a bear. After he had singed it, Young-Man said, "Grandmother, lend me your club."

"What do you wish to do with it? Have you seen someone doing something wrong?" asked Old-Woman.

She prepared two bowls of cooked meat. Then Young-Man said to Pretty-Woman-with-Red-Hair, "Ha ha! You are too experienced. You are accustomed to kill and eat people." He placed both bowls before her. He stuck the club up in the ground beside them. "If you fail to eat all the food, I shall strike you with this club," he said. He watched her to prevent her from going outside.

After a long while, she went out. She was a fast runner so she ran as swiftly as she could. But lo! She was still at the very edge of the house. Then she vomited. She kept this up a long time. Finally she vomited up a piece of ice. This it was that had caused her to eat people. After that she was all right. After that she ate what others ate. Some time later she bore a son. She named him Red-Horn.

"Aha! Grandmother, I have accomplished that for which I am intended," said Young-Man. "So now I am going to my spirit home. People can now prosper in this country. That is why I came."*

*This story was written during the fur-trade wars that the Winnebago people were involved in with the Algonquian tribes and the French from 1600 to 1640, when the culture was changing.

The
Captive Boy

Author unknown

Once there was a Ho-Chunk village that had existed for some time. At one period in its history, some enemies made a sudden attack on it and killed many of its inhabitants in an awful manner. The invaders spared a boy and carried him off to their own land. When they reached home, they gave this boy away to another person, who in turn parted with him, and so on till the boy had changed owners three times. When he fell into the possession of his fourth owner, he was allowed to stay with that master.

Later on, another marauding party brought a second boy who had been spared.* They gave this boy to the man who kept the first boy, requesting him to bring up both of them to maturity. Now these two boys became great friends. They became excellent hunters, following the example of their keeper.

At length, the boys reached the full stature of manhood and the adoptive father thus addressed them: "When boys become young men they always hunt game." So the youths began to go hunting on their own account, without being accompanied by the man. They killed a powerful animal on

---

Story collected by David Lee Smith from the
Anthropological Archives, Smithsonian Institution.

*Captive children were often incorporated into an enemy tribe to replace children who had themselves been killed or taken captive by other tribes. This practice occurred in certain Great Lakes tribes.

almost every occasion. Consequently, the people came to invite the two youths to feasts.

At the first feast, one man made a speech, saying that the two youths should be the first to eat. Just as he was saying that, the chief rose suddenly to his feet and walked out from the presence of the guests. This displeased the two youths. When they were invited to the second feast, another chief showed them a similar act of discourtesy, and in like manner behaved a third and a fourth chief, each at a different feast. Such behavior made the two youths very angry.

By and by the fall came, and the people struck camp moving to another place. The two youths always kept together. Once when they had just camped for the night, they came to the place where a chief was. It was one of the chiefs who had insulted them. This chief was chopping firewood in the dense forest. When the youths became aware of his proximity, they conferred together, saying that they would kill him. When they approached him, they observed that the chief's knife was with him. They killed him, took his head, and started home.* Although they took revenge on all four chiefs by killing them, the people never found out.

At length it was summer, and on the return of the two youths to the camp a chief told them that they were slaves. Then the youths had another conference and they determined that they would go elsewhere, so they departed on the following morning. They traveled for ten days without eating anything. At length they came unexpectedly to a river; it is said that this stream was the Missouri River.

In a very little while, they came suddenly upon a village. One of the two youths said to the other, "Friend, remain here. Let me go first to that place. After my return, let us go together."

"Agreed," replied the other.

In the evening, the first youth went to the village. His friend awaited his return all night long at the base of a tree.

*The Winnebagos believed that if the head was separated from the body, the spirit of the dead person would find no rest.

Just as the morning dawned, his friend returned and the two went together.

Just as they reached the first lodge, a man came out, and the two youths seized him, one standing on each side of him. When they did so, the man howled, giving a sign of alarm. This caused all the sleepers to awake. Out of the lodges they poured, surrounding the two youths, who struck their chests again and again without intermission, signifying by this that they were then with their own people. At length they ceased doing that. Just then, some of the people went after an old man, and when they had returned with him, he addressed the two youths saying, "Of what people are you?"

Then one of the youths replied, "We are the Ho-Chunk."* And the old man reported the words to the people. The two youths proceeded to give an account of themselves, saying that when they were small, war parties had attacked their village, carrying off the two boys, each at a different time. The old man repeated their words, and the people believed them.

At first, the people were at a loss what to do with the two youths, but at length they decided they should be received again into the Ho-Chunk Tribe. So the two took wives there and dwelt in very good lodges.

---

*Ho-Chunk is what the Winnebagos call themselves. The name Winnebago was given to them by the Europeans.

The
Rabbit
and the
Grasshoppers

By Oliver LaMere, Bear Clan

There was once a village of grasshoppers who stole tobacco from man. Grandmother Earth said, "My grandson, let us go to the grasshopper's village. Ma-ona gave tobacco to man and the grasshoppers have taken it all away. Therefore let us go."

"Yes!" said Rabbit.

So Rabbit and his grandmother went together and soon were close to the grasshopper's village. When they were on the outskirts of the village, the old woman said, "My grandson, do what you think best." Rabbit yelled, and when he yelled the whole earth shook.

The grasshoppers said, "Wa! A very bad god is coming. We shall be destroyed." So the grasshopper chief took some tobacco and gave it to Rabbit. He, in turn, gave it to his grandmother, and the old woman put it in her sack.

And Rabbit yelled a second time. He shook the earth with his mouth more than before. And the grasshoppers said, "Hau! it will be bad. Give him tobacco again as before." So the chief of the grasshoppers, having taken some tobacco, gave it again to Rabbit. "Well, Grandmother, here it is. Take it. It will be easy to get the rest."

So Rabbit yelled again. And when he yelled, he shook the earth with his mouth more than ever. And the grasshoppers said, "Hau! It is very bad. He is coming very close. Hau!

Story collected by David Lee Smith.

Give him tobacco as before." Again the grasshopper chief took some tobacco and gave it to Rabbit.

Rabbit said, "Here is some more tobacco. Well, Grandmother, it will be very easy to get the rest of the tobacco."

Well, Grandson, that will do." And she took the tobacco.

When Rabbit yelled again, the whole world shook worse than before. Then all the grasshoppers flew upward. The grasshoppers took some tobacco in their mouths and flew away. Therefore, they are just as if they chewed tobacco and something dark yellow comes out of their mouths.

The old woman, taking the tobacco, scattered it over the earth. And all the seed came up and it grew on the earth. So man again had tobacco.

Selfish
Woman

By Pat Smith Medina, Thunder Clan

A Winnebago woman was filling water bags near the stream when she heard a voice from the water. The voice said, "Woman, woman, do you seek true love?"

The woman thought that she was imagining the voice, because she did desire true love. She spoke out loud, "Yes, I do seek true love. Will you help me find it?"

There was no answer. She did not see Ugly-Fish, who once was a man, floating in the water. Shortly thereafter, the woman married a great warrior of the highest clan. All spoke of her with admiration and said she would bear him many sons. The woman did bear children, but only daughters. She sat by the river again. She heard the voice say to her, "Woman, I can help you bear your husband a son."

The woman, in disbelief, replied, "You are only a voice in the stream."

Ugly-Fish lay under a branch hidden from the woman. He said, "If you send your daughters to the stream each day to visit me, I will grant you a son and your husband will love you forever more."

The woman was in great despair and feared that her husband would eventually find a woman to bear him a son. She quickly agreed to send her daughters to the stream each day.

Many moons passed and she never was blessed with a son. Her beautiful daughters all grew up to be very bad and many of the tribe's people spoke poorly of them. The tribe accused the woman of failing to raise her daughters properly.

The woman's husband took her sister as his new wife, and the sister gave birth to many sons.

A woman must never be selfish. She should always be grateful for the blessing of any children, for Ma-ona bestowed this honor upon women.

Selfish
Woman

Winnebago Names

By Pat Smith Medina, Thunder Clan

When Earth-Maker created people to live on this land, he gave them clans in which to belong. There were twelve separate clans. All clans and their members had individual duties and responsibilities to the tribe. Each clan member was given his or her own name.

Clan names were given to individuals (usually by a male relative) at a feast or special ceremony. The names had to reflect the person's personality and wellbeing. Each name also had to originate from the person's own particular clan.

If a woman from the Thunder Clan, for example, had a son, and assuming that the boy's father had no clan because of his tribe,* the son would be of the Thunder Clan. The boy would be named by his male relative. The name to reflect on his life or personality might be Wa-kan-ja-cici-ga, or Bad Thunder-Bird—a name clearly associated with the Thunder-Bird Clan.

That is how it has always been.

---

*Some tribes—for example, the Sioux—did not have clans in their social structure.

The
Journey

By Rita Sharpback, Buffalo Clan

Brother Rabbit was always a mischievous person. He was never evil but came close to it at times. Grandmother Rabbit, however, was very patient with him and tried to steer him the right way.

In the prime of his life, Brother Rabbit was killed by a giant monster that stalked near the lake. Brother Rabbit journeyed to the Milky Way and came to the old woman in the fork of the road. She asked Brother Rabbit, "Did you do well in the world you left?"

He at first wanted to say yes, but was afraid of the punishment for lying. He uttered, "No, I was not a good person there. I know I hurt many people; especially my grandmother, who tried her hardest to help me."

The old woman on the Milky Way said, "If this that you have told be the truth, you will be stopped here from going on your journey." She then pushed Brother Rabbit off the Milky Way.

When he returned to earth, Brother Rabbit was a better person. He had no recollection of what happened before, but would receive glimpses of his former life in his dreams. He encountered different landscapes and knew that he had been there before. Still, he was not a genuinely good being. Brother Rabbit retained many of his former weaknesses. Once more, Brother Rabbit was killed by the monster who stalked near the lake. He met the old woman on the Milky

Way again and she asked the same question as before, "Did you do well in the world that you left?"

Again, Rabbit answered, "I tried, but am afraid to say that I was not a good person." Again, the old woman pushed him off the Milky Way.

In his next life, Brother Rabbit was indeed a good person. He always helped people in need and rarely thought of himself. He did good deeds for many years. Rabbit died in his sleep one night and found himself on the journey to the Milky Way. He met the old woman at the fork and she asked, "Brother Rabbit, did you do well in the world you left?"

He could now answer with great joy, "Yes, I was a good person."

With this, she let him continue on his journey. He came to a circle of wigwams and there was his grandmother. Grandmother Rabbit said, "Grandson, I have waited for you for a long time. Come, we must speak with your other relatives who have made the journey."

How
Skunks
Came To Be

By Keely Bassette, Water Spirit Clan,
and Rita Sharpback, Buffalo Clan

Once long ago there was a beautiful Indian woman. She was very unusual and was thought to have special and unique powers because she was born with white hair. Men from all over would come and try to marry her, but she wanted none of them. Instead, she was content to sit by a clear stream and stare at her reflection. She also loved the smell of sweet flowers and would rub her skin and hair with their leaves.

One day a particularly ugly young man came and asked for her hand in marriage and C-ga* just laughed and laughed because he was so ugly. Now the ugly man really wasn't an ordinary man; he was Turtle.

Turtle was very angry with C-ga, because she had snubbed him. He shed his repugnant outer skin and shouted to her, "C-ga, you were once blessed, but now you will become an animal."

C-ga screamed and her body changed until she was a small, black animal with a big, white stripe down her back. Every time people would come around her, she would spray them with a horrific smell. That's how skunks became skunks.

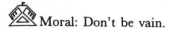 Moral: Don't be vain.

*C-ga means thirdborn daughter.

Why
the Owl
Hunts at Night

By Jennifer A. Smith, Thunder Clan

One day, Owl said to Grandmother, "Grandmother, can I go hunting?"

Grandmother said, "Go and get arrows from your uncle's lodge, but do not touch any of the medicine lying about, for it is very evil and bad things will happen to you."

But Owl was very curious and dipped his arrows into some of the medicine thinking this would give him power.

Grandmother told him to hunt only in the daytime, but thinking he now had power, he went out at night. Owl thought the night would make him even more powerful. He soon came upon an elk. He shot his arrow into the elk. The elk fell over, but when he went to pull his arrow out, a flash of light blinded him. Confused, Owl made it home and Grandmother said, "You have done an evil thing. For this, you must hunt only at night. Only then will you be able to see to hunt your prey."

This is why people see an owl hunting only at night and not during the day.

The
Greedy Ones

By Jennifer A. Smith, Thunder Clan

At the beginning of time, the animals ruled over all. Soon, however, they began to argue and fight amongst themselves. This continued on until all the animals had either killed each other or had run off into the darkness.

When one animal was left, he felt alone. So he, too, left this enormous place. He wandered about until he was exhausted. Soon he fell asleep hoping he would never wake. He felt bad, for he was the one who had caused all the fighting in the first place. He then started praying to Earth-Maker for forgiveness. Earth-Maker said, "For what you have done you must pay the price. You must roam the earth for a period of time and you shall never grow tall. For causing your brothers to fight and kill one another, you will let them hunt you, and you must not run."

The small creature agreed, but soon broke his promise to Earth-Maker. He ran from his brothers, the eagle and the hawk.

That is why animals had their power taken away and they are hunted by humans. The small creature, however, is always hunted by his own kind, his brothers and his sisters—the animals. For this, the mouse must survive on little or no food and live forever in hiding.

Why
Spider
Has Eight Eyes

By Joi St. Cyr, Bear Clan

Being a very wise spirit, Ma-ona saw the need for a being to watch over all he had created.

First Ma-ona asked for Turtle's help. But Turtle was so short-legged, he had great difficulty seeing far and wide.

Second, Ma-ona asked for Crow's help. Crow was able to see far and wide, but was not happy merely to watch. Crow cawed orders to every being and every thing.

Third, Ma-ona asked for Bear's help. Bear was able to see far and wide when he stood on his hind legs or climbed tall trees. Bear used his voice wisely, but his temper was unpredictable.

Fourth, Ma-ona asked Spider. She could see far and wide because of her great climbing ability. She could only watch—as her voice was heard only by Ma-ona. Spider was neither angry nor happy—she just was. To help her in her watch, Ma-ona gave her eight eyes—one eye for each of the four directions and one eye for each of the other directions.

How
Fire Came to the
Winnebagos

By David Lee Smith, Thunder Clan

When Ma-ona first created the Winnebagos, they had no
fire to cook their food and keep them warm. That was until
the birth of Little Brother. Little Brother was born when the
snow was deep and the winter winds cold. Grandfather
named him Snow-Walker.

As the seasons went by, Snow-Walker grew into a young
man. One night while he was asleep, he was called into the
heavens by the powerful Thunderbirds. The Thunderbird
who guarded the north spoke to Snow-Walker first, "My
grandson, years ago Ma-ona created your people from the
dirt within his nose, and over the years you have done well."
The Thunderbird who guarded the south spoke next, "Our
brother Turtle was sent down in the beginning to get rid of
all the two-legged creatures that threatened mankind, but in
the process he made the people war against each other."
When a deep voice spoke to him from the west, Snow-Walker
turned and faced the Thunderbird who guarded the sunset.
"When Turtle was sent down, he carried a sacred
Thunderbird war club with him," said the Thunderbird
who guarded the west. "After Turtle destroyed the two-
legged people, the Thunderbird war club was stolen from
him by a fish-god of the sea."

Snow-Walker next turned to the east when he heard
thunder coming from that direction. "In order to get back
our war club, you must answer the riddle the fish-god will
ask of you." After a few moments, the Thunderbird from

the sunrise continued, "If you recover our war club, we will grant you one wish, and if you fail to recover our property, you will spend the rest of your days as a fish." Then the Thunderbirds all laid their wings on Snow-Walker and said in one voice, "Go now our grandson, and think of what will keep your people warm through the winter." With a flash of lightning, Snow-Walker awoke to find himself all alone.

Hours later, he found himself on the shores of a great lake. And according to tribal legends, this was the waters that held the stolen Thunderbird war club. After fasting for four days, Snow-Walker walked into the waters and was gone from human sight. Days later, he approached the gate to the homeland of the fish god, and the gate was guarded by two giant two-headed catfish. When Snow-Walker demanded entrance, they refused him. But Snow-Walker wasn't about to give up. He reached into his bag and brought out a flute. After sitting on a seashell, he started to play a water-spirit song. This song seemed to have the right effect, because both of the catfish went to sleep and Snow-Walker continued his journey.

After walking for hours, he accepted a ride on the back of a sea horse and promised the sea horse that he would one day bring him above land so he could serve his people. After saying good-bye to his newfound friend, he entered the cave and home of the great sea-god. Snow-Walker found himself in a great tunnel, guarded by every known fish that Ma-ona created at the beginning of the world. And at the end of this tunnel was the powerful sea-god. He spoke in a thundering voice, "Welcome to my domain, little man. What can I do to help you?" The young man said, "I am the Snow-Walker, and I have come after the war club of the Thunderbirds."

The sea-god answered him, "Ah yes—one born of the snows and sired by the Thunderbirds. I have been waiting for you." After taking a long look into the watery eyes of the sea-god, Snow-Walker said, "I come to answer the riddle of the war club, so that I may take it back to its true owners." The sea-god seemed to smile and said, "If you cannot answer the riddle, I will release all the sea animals on your people at tomorrow's dawn, and they shall finish the job that the giants failed to do. And moreover," he continued, "you shall be my servant for all your lifetimes."

To Snow-Walker, time seemed to stop here in the sea bottom as the sea-god said in a low, pounding voice, "What devours without mouth both flesh and plant . . . and grows more ravenous, until at last, given a drink of water . . . it dies?" Then he said, "Speak your answer quickly, snow-being, or . . ." Snow-Walker answered him, "The answer is fire." The sea-god seemed startled at first then said, "By all the spirit beings—you are right. But how can a snow-being like you, untutored in magic . . . ?" Snow-Walker replied, "The Indian mind is trained to hunt truth through the mask made by words, Fish. Now keep your vow."

The sea-god reached under his right fin and said, "Here take the war club and begone from my domain before I change my mind and eat you." Snow-Walker took the Thunder-weapon and returned to his world on dry land. After climbing to the tallest hill that he could see, he sat down and prayed. Then he hit the war club four times on hard rock and his whole world seemed to explode. When he again woke up, he stood and looked around him. In place of the Thunderbird war club, a small fire was burning. In all his young years on earth, he always wanted to know what fire was used for. Now he knew, for the Thunderbirds had finally given fire to the Winnebagos.

From that day forward they never were cold again.

How
Valleys and
Ravines Came to Be

By David Lee Smith, Thunder Clan

Long ago, when the Creator wished for earth, Earth came
into existence. The Creator looked on Earth and he liked
what he had created. Then the Creator made beings out of
the dirt of his nose. He threw them down to earth and
breathed life into them. The Thunder People were some of
the beings he made, as were the War People and others.

During the early days, the people and animals could run
around Earth very quickly and easily, for there were no hills
or valleys. All was flat. Animals enjoyed grazing and the
hunting was good. Many animals were killed.

A young man named Wa-kan-jagi-ci-ci-ga lived alone with
his grandmother, for his mother and father were no longer
alive. He was looked on favorably by his uncles, who were
the powerful Thunder People. One day, Wa-kan-jagi-ci-ci-ga
told his grandmother he was going hunting. So he made
preparations and set out for the hunt. The Thunder People
watched him prepare, and they were pleased.

Wa-kan-jagi-ci-ci-ga walked for four days. On the fourth
day he saw a small herd of elk, but they ran off while he was
too far away to kill one. He then saw two deer, but they also
ran before he was close enough to make a kill. Finally he saw
a village and walked to the village.

Now in this village lived an evil chief who had a very
wicked son. They were disliked by all other Indians and the
spirits themselves. Now the chief's son noticed Wa-kan-jagi-
ci-ci-ga while he was still far away and alerted the people of

the village to prepare for an enemy invasion. As Wa-kan-jagi-ci-ci-ga approached the village, the wicked son shot him full of arrows and Wa-kan-jagi-ci-ci-ga died.

The Thunder People saw what had happened and were enraged. They fasted, painted their faces black, and began wandering the earth striking it with their clubs and in this matter created the valleys and ravines we see today. The evil chief and his son fled for safety into the underworld and became earthworms, the lowest of the creator's creatures. They became food for the fish.

Part Four

LEGENDS OF
THE WINNEBAGO
PEOPLE

The Morning Star

By Louis L. Meeker

After Ma-ona had made Earth, he made a man. While the man lay by the fire to dry, one of his legs cracked off. So he was called Wah-reh-ksan-ke-ka, or Man-with-Only-One-Leg. He was cast aside. Therefore, deformed children are said to be no good.

This occurred on top of the sky. The fire was the sun. Wah-reh-ksan-ke-ka fell to the earth and made much trouble. Some say Ma-ona just happened to drop him and one leg broke off when he fell.

Then Ma-ona made another and said, "Open your eyes and see. Open your ears and hear. I will call you Koo-noo-ga, or First-Boy. I will give you Hotchahngara words. When you speak, talk to me. Talk Hotchahngara." It is our duty to speak our language. It is the oldest tongue.

Ma-ona gave Koo-noo-ga only the short words, but more were made by putting many together. When we give anyone anything we say "gah," so all names end in *ga*. Everything has a trunk; therefore, all common words end in *ra*, or trunk. The second word ends in *na*, which is the same thing, so not to say *ra* so often.

Touching Koo-noo-ga and the parts of his body, Ma-ona gave them names. Koo-noo-ga and his brothers were eight. Those who say there were ten count the name of his manhood, Wah-teh-gho-ga, and the name of Wah-reh-ksan-ke-ka.

Story collected by David Lee Smith.

The names of the first four were Koo-noo-ga, Hay-noo-ga, Ha-gay-ga, and Nah-ghee-ga, but after the eighth person, the latter was Nah-ghee-gheh-deh-ga, which means big Nah-ghee-ga. (Whether or not the other names underwent a similar change does not appear.) These are family names to this day.

The names of the other four were Koo-noo-gho-no-neenk, Hay-noo-gho-no-neenk, Ha-gay-gho-no-neenk, and Nah-ghee-gho-no-neenk. These names mean little Koo-noo-ga, and so forth. They are the ancestors of the eight clans: Wah-neenk-hee-kee-kah-ratch—Birds; Gheh-hee-kee-kah-ratch—Hills; Honch-hee-kee-kah-ratch—Bears; Wah-kchay-ghee-hee-kee-kah-ratch—Buffaloes; Ho-hee-kee-kah-ratch—Fish; Chah-hee-kee-kah-ratch—Deer or Elk; Shunk-chunk-hee-kee-kah-ratch—Wolves; Wah-kang-hee-kee-kah-ratch—Thunder.

Koo-noo-ga went hunting and tracked a raccoon until it went over the cliff into a deep gorge. Koo-noo-ga fell over the cliff, but he lodged in the branches of a large tree that grew high up on the side of the bank very near the top.

After many hours, when Koo-noo-ga did not return, his brothers went forth in search of him and followed his trail until they came to the place where he was hanging. They looked over and saw Koo-noo-ga. They discussed how they could rescue him and one said in one way and another said in another, until it at last came the turn of Nah-ghee-gho-no-neenk, who said, "We will make ourselves fast together with our carrying straps and so form a chain of ourselves by which we can bring him up." And it was done in this manner.

Koo-noo-ga said, "My brothers, do not be afraid of any man nor of any animal nor of anything whatever. I myself am *gho pena*—the good and the wise, mysterious being, the wisest and bravest and mightiest—and into whatever danger any one of you or even I myself should come, by my might and wisdom and mystery we shall always be safe in the end. There is another man besides ourselves; he thinks himself so wise and brave and mighty that he claims to be more mysterious than I, but be not afraid of him."

Many times the long camp trailed to the same tree the animal that Koo-noo-ga had followed. At length, Ha-gay-ga or Hay-noo-ga went to the lower end of the gorge to come up the gorge to the tree where the animal made its home. And when the day had passed and the night also and the next morning came, Hah-gay-ga set forth in quest of Hay-noo-ga. And when the day had passed away and the night also and the morning came, Nah-ghee-ga set forth in quest of Hah-gay-ga. When the day had passed and the night also and the morning had come again and again, at length it came the turn of Ha-ghe-gho-no-neenk to go in search of the animal that none of them had captured and also to learn why none of his brothers returned.

Nah-ghee-gho-no-neenk followed the trail of his brothers. He, as well as they, wore snowshoes, and when he had gone far down the gorge to where it grew wider and its banks sloped, he entered, turned, and sought the spot where the animal made its den. He found the tree to be hollow. In the opening at the bottom, a fire had been recently kindled. Nearby, in a row, were six pairs of snowshoes stuck in the snow and standing upright.

Nah-ghee-gho-no-neenk was weary. His feet were cold and wet. Before long he had built a fire in the same place, taken off his snowshoes, and stood them up in the snow by those of his brother, and seated himself to warm his feet at the fire. He was just going to sleep as he sat when he was roused by a noise that he first thought was made by the animal descending in the tree on account of the smoke that was made by the fire he had kindled.

But turning his eyes upward, he beheld Wah-reh-ksan-ke-ka coming down out of the sky. Quickly fitting an arrow to his bow, he shot, but without effect. Again, and a third time, he discharged an arrow with the same result, but the fourth stuck into the side of Wah-reh-ksan-ke-ka. The arrow, however, did not kill him, so poor Nah-ghee-gho-no-neenk was soon in the grasp of his enemy and born away to his own place.

"In all my life I have never had anyone hurt me that way before," said Wah-reh-ksan-ke-ka. Then he whipped Nah-ghee-gho-no-neenk with briars until, in mortal agony, the little man cried and sang:

Wah het ho no gra
He nih sjih
Na sha na
Wa ne gho pe na
He sha rah
Wa teh ho ne gra
He nih sjih
Na sha na
Wa ne gho pe na
He sha rah
Wa teh ho ne gra
He nih sjih*

Now the first word meant Koo-noo-ga, to whom he sang. The second word means "my eldest older brother," the third, "you yourself alone," the forth, on to "a good, wise spirit or angel" and the last, "so you said." It was as if he had reproached Koo-noo-ga by calling upon him by name and saying, "Oh, oldest of all my brothers, you said that you alone are a mighty, wise, and mysterious being."

Koo-noo-ga heard him clear around the world and came to him over the sky. He found poor Nah-ghee-gho-no-neenk bound and being used to stop the entrance to Wah-reh-ksan-ke-ka's tent, to keep out the cold.

Koo-noo-ga remained as a guest of his brother's captor during the night and, when asked to tell a story to pass away the time, he excused himself on the grounds of not knowing any story and urged his host to tell one. So Wa-reh-ksan-ke-ka told how he had strangled Koo-noo-ga's brothers, taken

---

*In the chant, he is asking forgiveness for any sorrow he may have caused.

off their skins, inflated them with air, and preserved the flesh for food. He exhibited the lifelike but empty skins of Koo-noo-ga's brothers, standing, as they were, on guard around the tent.

"And why did you not kill Na-ghee-gho-no-neenk also?" asked Koo-noo-ga.

"He is small and would make but little food," was the reply, "so I preserved him alive, to torture him for causing me pain with his arrow. In all my life no one has ever hurt me in that way until now."

"And now," said Koo-noo-ga, "I have come to kill you, for the cries of my little brother came to me clear around the world."

But it was now morning, and Wa-reh-ksan-ke-ka proposed that they should determine who had the greatest powers by playing ball, or shinny, an aboriginal game in which a block of wood is struck with a club, the players each having a long club and either striking in turn or competing for a chance to strike.

Koo-noo-ga acquiesced and his opponent delivered the first blow. But instead of striking the block of wood, he knocked off the head of Koo-noo-ga, which flew up to the sky and passed through it into the presence of Ma-ona, He-Who-Made-the-World. Before it fell, the head asked permission to kill Wah-reh-ksan-ke-ka, but received no reply. So it fell to the earth and fixed itself on the neck where it fit exactly as before.

It was now Koo-noo-ga's turn to strike. He did with his opponent exactly as had been done with himself. When the head of Wah-reh-ksan-ke-ka asked permission of Ma-ona to kill Koo-noo-ga, Ma-ona did not reply. This was repeated until the head of each had been knocked off and flown upward through the sky three times, receiving no response from Ma-ona and attaching itself again to the still living body.

But when Koo-noo-ga's head ascended for the fourth time and asked for permission to kill his antagonist, Ma-ona said, "*ho jah,*" that is to say, "all right." So when the head of

Wah-reh-ksan-ke-ka was in the sky for the fourth time, before it fell, Koo-noo-ga pushed the body away. So perished Wah-reh-ksan-ke-ka.

Wah-reh-ksan-ke-ka had many wives, and some say that his children were adopted by Nah-ghee-gho-no-neenk to be the Spirit Clan. Nah-ghee-gho-no-neenk became the morning star, but his brothers became the clouds.

Each of the bothers married the sister of another brother, except Nah-ghee-gho-no-neenk, who never married. So members of the same family or clan do not intermarry. Some say Koo-noo-ga brought his brothers to life and they married afterward. Others say they were married before.

The
Dogs of
the Chief's Son

By W. C. McKern

It happened in a Winnebago village. The chief had one son and he had two dogs. One was a black dog and the other was spotted black and white. One day the chief's son went hunting. His father advised him not to take his wife. "If anything happens to you, don't come home without her," the chief said, "for then the people would despise you." But the chief's son took his wife and the two dogs with him.

They came to the hunting place and set up a lodge there. It was the fall of the year. Although the man hunted constantly he had no success. There came a light snowfall. "Now the hunting ought to be good," the man thought. But there was no sign of any game. Every day he hunted all day long, but got nothing. The supply of food was getting very low.

The chief's son loved his two dogs very much. He awoke in the middle of the night. There was a noise; it was someone talking. He had never heard those voices before, he thought. Then he realized that the two dogs were talking together. He could understand every word they said.* Black-Dog was older and larger than Spotted-Dog. Black-Dog said, "Younger brother, I have failed to help

Story collected by David Lee Smith.

*The miracle here was not that the two dogs could talk to each other, but that the man could understand them. Winnebagos believed that all animals could talk.

find any game. You are younger than I am. Why don't you try to find something? Our brother [the chief's son] needs help."

Spotted-Dog said, "Oh, I could find something if I wanted to, all right, but our sister-in-law [the wife of the chief's son] treats me badly. No, I am sorry, but I don't feel like helping. She treats me like a dog."

Then Black-Dog said, "You are always thinking of yourself. How about our older brother? He has always treated us very well. We should scare up some game on his account."

"Well," said Spotted-Dog, "I could do that easily if he would give me the rest of the food supply, but I can't hunt without food."

The man awoke at daylight. He roused his wife and told her to prepare what remained of the food supply. She did as she was told. When it was cooked, the man told her to put it in a bowl. This she did and brought it to him. Then he cooled the food, stirring it with a spoon, after which he gave it to the two dogs. Then the man spoke to the dogs. He said, "Brothers, since you have lived with me, I have always treated you right. I have taken good care of you, and brought you up to be my companions. The food we had is all gone; I am giving the last of it to you now. I shall not eat a bite of it. I wish that you would go and find some more food, so that we might eat again. I am hungry now." Then he gave the food to the dogs, and they ate it.

After eating, the dogs left the lodge. Immediately, Spotted-Dog was away. Soon they heard him barking a short distance from the camp. The man had hunted at that spot many times and caught nothing. This time, however, he saw that Spotted-Dog had found a very large bear. This kind of bear we call *watok*. He has a double nest, it is said, part for the body and part for the head. They killed the bear right in his nest, and he was so large that they could not pull him out. So the man called his wife to help. It was still early in the morning, so she cooked some bear meat for their breakfast. The dogs also were fed again.

After that, they again hunted. Spotted-Dog located another bear. The chief's son killed a deer. From that time on they found plenty of game. They secured a good supply of meat. The man and his wife made a rack on which to place the dry meat for safe keeping.

Once again, the chief's son awoke in the middle of the night. Again he heard the dogs talking together. Black-Dog spoke to his younger brother. "There is a fire coming this way," he said—referring to an enemy. "You can run faster than I can, younger brother; I wish that you would spy on them."

"All right, I can do that," said Spotted-Dog, "but I would like to have something to eat before I go." So the man got up and built a fire. Then he told his wife to prepare some food. When it was ready, he gave the food to the dogs.

After eating, Spotted-Dog started out. He made a four-nights' journey. There he came upon the enemy. He heard the leader say that they were going after a man, his wife, and two dogs. This the leader told his followers after they had filled his pipe and asked for his plans.

The dog returned to the chief's son. He arrived home just before daylight.* He told the man that the enemy were four days distant. "They are coming after us, "he said. The chief's son then said to Spotted-Dog, "Take the news back to the village." Spotted-Dog said, "All right, but first give me something to eat." So the man fed him again.

The village was also a four-days' journey away. Spotted-Dog arrived there one morning. The people knew that the chief's son had two dogs. They were alarmed to see only one dog return. They thought that all had been killed but his dog.

Spotted-Dog entered the chief's lodge. He licked the chief's hands and whined. The chief could not understand what the dog tried to say. It was necessary to consult a *cunkhitenahkun*. They sent after an old woman who had this

---

*The dog demonstrates his spirit power by traveling a four-day's journey in one night.

power. She talked with Spotted-Dog. She said to him, "Your people are anxious to know why you returned home all alone. Have your brothers and sister been killed by an enemy?"

Spotted-Dog said, "I have been trying to tell them, but they do not understand me. Stranger enemies are coming. I was sent here to get you to come and help my brothers. They are waiting there for the enemy to come. Give me something to eat and I shall return to help them. Follow my tracks and you will be guided to the place where we are."

So the chief sent two callers to tell all the people. They made preparations and started right away. Each man took extra moccasins with him. Spotted-Dog finished eating. Then he started on his return journey. He arrived there that same day. The war party only arrived after two days of unbroken traveling. Spotted-Dog spied on the enemy to find out just where they were. Black-Dog said, "Our enemy's dream will not come true. I have more power than they have."

When the reinforcements arrived, they were given plenty of food from the hunter's supplies. Then they prepared to fight. There was snow on the ground. Spotted-Dog said that the enemy would come the next morning. A great number of the enemy was approaching. It was decided to set a trap for them. So they hid on either side of the approach to camp.

The dogs were to cry the signal to start fighting; this was because the enemy would pay no attention to the dogs. The dogs were to cry from four places. They call this kind of ambush *waikecen*. As soon as all the enemy came within the wings of the trap, the dogs cried four times as instructed. Then those lying in wait started to shoot. The enemy knew then that they were trapped. They were tired from their long journey. Those attacking them had had plenty of food and rest and were fresh for the battle. That is why they killed the enemy easily. They were exterminated.

Then the victors started for home. They carried with them all the meat supplies and the scalps of the enemy. From that time on the two dogs were very useful. Black-Dog used to know when an enemy was coming and Spotted-Dog acted as a spy. He was also clever at hunting.

When Black-Dog was real old, he said to Spotted-Dog, "Brother, I am going to leave you and go to that place whence I came. I urge you to remain with our brother, the chief's son, and to help him as long as you live. When you, too, are ready to go, you must come to my place." Black-Dog was *cunktcen kwilukana*, the wolf spirit.

The
Dog That
Became a Panther

By W. C. McKern

This young man was a chief's son. He took no interest in hunting and wars. He preferred to go about visiting with the people. His dog was small and light-colored. The man was never known to mistreat his dog.

Some young men planned to go hunting for deer. They thought that they would like to take along the chief's son, this young man who was never interested in hunting. They thought he would be useful as camp caretaker. So they invited him to come along. He accepted their invitation. They hunted for several days.

One day they discovered men's tracks near the camp. These they observed while returning from hunting. Some said, "Let us return to the village without going back to the camp. Some enemy awaits us there. If they kill this fellow, that is but one. Let the rest of us escape." So they returned home without telling the chief's son about the strange tracks.

The chief's son was left alone with his dog. He waited for the hunters until it was very late, but they did not come. The dog spoke. The chief's son thought that it was strange that a dog should talk Ho-Chunk. He could understand perfectly everything that the dog said. He told the chief's son what had taken place and all that had been said by the hunters. "Do not worry, my brother," said the dog, "they shall not

Story collected by David Lee Smith.

kill us. You need not fight. I'll watch over you tonight. Go right to sleep."

But the man was afraid to sleep. The dog kept going out and coming in again. "It is nearly dawn now," he said. "Do not go outside when you hear their war whoop. Stay in the lodge. I am going out to fight them when they come, but do not attempt to look at me."

Soon after that, the dog went out and the fight began. The dog came into the lodge from time to time during the battle. The fight was still raging at midday. Once in a while, the chief's son heard a war whoop outside. He wondered about that. He thought it would be fun to look and see what was happening, but the dog had told him not to look at him while he was fighting.

Nevertheless, the chief's son peeked out the door of the lodge. That was when the dog gave a low cry and ran from the enemy. He came running into the lodge. There was an arrow through his forepaw.* He told the man to pull it out. Then the dog said, "That settles it; they have me started now. I am going out and I will finish it. If you wish to join in the fight, just follow me. No harm will come to you."

The chief's son decided to help in the fight, so he left the lodge. The dog was there fighting. He had changed into an angry panther. He was ferocious. He threw himself at the enemy with ever increasing rage. The man took his place in the fight beside the panther. Then the panther said, "It is good of you to help me out. We'll soon exterminate these fellows." Before long they had killed them all.

Then the panther said, "Now we can return home. We shall take all these scalps with us. Those who returned to the village have reported that we were both killed." So they took the scalps and journeyed homeward. The dog remained in the form of a panther.

When they came to the village, everyone was much astonished at seeing them. Those hunters who had returned

*This injury resulted from the fact that the chief's son looked at the fighting dog contrary to the latter's instructions.

without them were told by their parents of the great wrong they had done. They had been afraid to fight and they had deserted the chief's son. Then they had lied, saying that he was dead.

The panther now told the chief's son, "It is not proper for me to live with you now. I shall stay here in the woods. I shall know if any of the enemy are coming and will always be on hand to help you." After that, the panther would always report to the chief's son the approach of an enemy party. The chief's son would go out to engage them in battle. So all looked up to him as a brave warrior. Whenever the chief's son wished to hunt deer, the panther would join him and together they would kill great quantities of game. Thus he gained the reputation of a great hunter.

"Now the time has come for me to leave," said the panther, "but whenever you wish to see me and talk with me, I shall meet you at a certain place. There I shall be with you." This is the agreement they made. Then the panther went away, and the people of the village saw him no more.

How
the Two Divisions
of the Winnebagos
Came Together

By Soloman Longtail, Wolf Clan

There once was a village of Winnebagos. The chief lived there. He ruled over all the people of that village. They did just what he asked them to do. One day a war party started with his consent.

Now this chief had four daughters and two sons. The old man said to his older son, "Young men of your age generally fast and go out to the woods and pray that some great spirit may bless them; but you have never done what people of your age are accustomed to do."

It was the custom in the old times that he who returned with a scalp should be given a wampum belt as a prize.* This he had to give to one of his sisters.

The young man, the older of the two brothers, went on a warpath. When the members of the warpath came back, he was the third of those who had taken a scalp. When Winnebagos return from a warpath, they generally march through the village with the scalps suspended from poles.† While they were thus marching through the village, the old

---

Story collected by David Lee Smith.

*This story is from the postcontact period for the Winnebagos. The Winnebagos never scalped other people until they were paid to do so by the early French people in the Upper Great Lakes region.

† This is a postcontact practice. In the earlier days, the Winnebagos believed that separating the head from the body would also separate the spirit from the dead person's body. This would cause the spirit to wander

chief saw his son, the third in the line. So he made fun of him, and said, "As old as I am, if I were to go on the warpath, I should come back the first; and if I should go, my sisters would march around the village with the first prize." The young man felt hurt, and walked out of the ranks, homeward. When he got home, his mother had his meal ready for him, which she had cut into chunks and put into a wooden bowl. The dish was set before the young man.

Before he had taken anything, the father came in, and taking some ashes he threw some into the dish. The boy did not eat anything. Four times war parties started out, but only at the fourth time did the boy come home first. He did not eat anything at that time. Even on the return of the fourth expedition, the father made fun of the young man. When he arrived home, the father again threw ashes into his food. Then the young man took his blanket and wrapped himself in it, covering his head, and he sat down and said not a word.

As he was lying down, he thought of his father's actions. He thought that his father did not like him and he preferred to die rather than to live. He went away toward the wilderness, taking his best clothing and bow and arrows, and blackened his face every morning. He wanted to die.

He traveled four days, running all the time. Then he came to a village on the morning of the fifth day. It was just about sunrise when he came to the village. It was foggy. He went up on a hill. When he got there, he saw the village lying underneath. He saw the long pole that stood in front of the chief's house. When he first started from his home, he had made up his mind to die in the wilderness, but when he saw the village, he hated to go there and be killed. Then he remembered that he had intended to go to the wilderness to die, so he grew brave again and went to the chief's house. He put on his best clothes and marched toward the camp.

the world forever, never finding the way to the Spiritland. After contact with the French, the Winnebagos picked up the practice of carrying scalps, as other Great Lakes and Plains tribes did. The Winnebagos also believed that by taking a person's scalp they would take that person's spirit to serve them in the afterworld.

While he was mourning, the perspiration had trickled over his blackened face and made long streaks. Then he went and stood in front of the chief's house.

The house of the chief, in the olden days, had a shed supported on four forked tree stumps. While he was standing at the door of the house, the chief's youngest daughter was just coming out and when she saw this man standing in front of the door early in the morning, she screamed at the top of her voice. Then her father said, "What is the matter? Why are you yelling?"

She replied, "My brother is standing at the door." [Her brother had been buried the day before, and when a chief or any member of his family dies, the whole village generally mourns.]

The old man said, "Tell him to come in."

So they invited him in. As he walked, every one in the lodge looked at him, and noticed that he looked exactly like the dead person: his clothing was the same and his movements were the same. The old man then told the public crier to announce to the people of the village that his son had come to life again; that the women should comb their hair, paint themselves, and be joyful and happy as before. Then they sent for the partner of the boy who had died. They told him that his partner had come to life again.

In the old days, the chief's house had a scaffold in the rear on which the chief's son always slept. This scaffold was supported on four tree stumps and was about four feet from the ground, so that a little ladder was required to ascend to it.

Then the old chief talked to his son and said to him, "Whenever you want to go anywhere, let your sister and aunt know of it, because in this part of the world three, four, or even five pairs of moccasins would not last very long. They will make for you all you need to carry on a trip."

The young man was a very lively, swift hunter. When he did not want to hunt, he would kill a few deer. One night, his partner came home late in the evening and said, "Partner, I have just been notified that a party is going out

121

How
the Two
Divisions
of the
Winnebagos
Came Together

traveling, and they told me to tell some person about it, so I have come to tell you."

"All right!" was the answer.

The next day, as it was just getting dark, his partner came around again, and said, "They have already gone." So both struck out on the trail immediately. They had determined upon a place to meet and there they overtook the other members of the expedition.

On the warpath, it is customary for each person to fall in line in the order of his arrival at the meeting place. A certain distance must also be observed between him and the next person. No person was permitted under any circumstance to pass in front of those ahead of him. When resting, it was the custom to look in the direction from which they had been coming.

As two partners had come last, they were the last in line. Then the head warrior's nephew—the one who serves him—was told to count the number of men in the party. This he did, and found the expected number. "The whole party is here," he said.

Then the head warrior got up and said, "Follow me." They all got up but one. Now one man was lying on his belly and he did not get up when the others did.

Then someone said, "Who is that lying down?" A few looked down on this fellow, and they saw it was the chief's son—a very unusual thing among Indians.

So one of the party said, "Say, that is the prisoner we have." This he said jokingly. Some of the others heard this remark about the so-called prisoner, and they said, "Stop saying that, for we don't know who that prisoner is. He may be our protection."

Then they started to travel again. They traveled all night, until morning. Then the warrior told his nephew to take the war bundle and place it on the ground carefully and gently. Thereupon the head warrior arose and spoke. "Friends, I want to say something to you. Our chief's son is along with us, and he has only one pair of moccasins with him. We shall each of us have to give him one pair of ours." Everyone consented, and the chief's son had plenty to wear. Then they traveled again four days and four nights.

When day dawned, the old chief arose, and said, "I am going to appoint one of you to go and kill an enemy for me." So he took a handful of tobacco and walked up to an Indian named White-Eagle-Feather. White-Eagle-Feather took the tobacco and said, "You all know that I am the only one that can kill a man in the middle of his own village." The man that passed the tobacco around went to all the others, offering them the same, but they all refused.

123

How
the Two
Divisions
of the
Winnebagos
Came Together

When he came to the two who had joked about the so-called prisoner, they also refused, but added, "Give it to the prisoner we have." They passed it to him, and he said, "Ha ho, all right! I am willing to follow suit to what White-Eagle-Feather said, and I will also bring you the scalp of one who wears a medal around his neck."

Then these two started. Then the two men ran along all day until noon, when they came to a large rock, and White-Eagle-Feather said, "Here is the place where I usually sharpen my knife to cut the scalps of our enemies." Then they began to whet their knives on the rock. "Don't get too smooth an edge on your knife, but get a rough one, because you can cut the scalp off better," said White-Eagle-Feather. They traveled until sundown, and then they came to the village of their enemies. It was a very large village. They came up a long hill and looked down upon the village.

White-Eagle-Feather said, "I can stand up erect and look at them, but they cannot see me." He looked out to find the chief's lodge. The chief's son said and did everything that White-Eagle-Feather said and did. In the evening they went down toward the village and traveled all night among them, just as if they belonged there. They stayed until morning in front of the chief's house. The sun had come to the top of the trees.

Then two people came out of the chief's lodge. Each of the two Winnebagos then gave a war whoop and attacked the two that came out. The young chief killed his man first, scalped him, took his medal, and said to White-Eagle-Feather, "I am going."

White-Eagle-Feather joined him and together they ran through the heart of the village. They ran together quite leisurely. After a while they were pursued and the pursuers were gaining on them. White-Eagle-Feather made a jump or two and got ahead of the young man, and said, "Young man, I am going. Do the best you can."

The enemy was getting nearer and nearer. As the enemy was thus gaining upon them, the two were running westward, away from the enemy's camp. White-Eagle-Feather kept ahead of him, so that there were soon two hills between them. The two hills were a long distance apart, and the young chief took a spurt and ran as well as he could. Before White-Eagle-Feather got to the third hill, the young chief had overtaken him, and in passing he said, "Young man, they are gaining upon us. I am going." With that, he sped away.

In running they had circled all around the village, toward the direction in which they had entered. They traveled together all the time. White-Eagle-Feather had, up to then, been the only person who had been able to enter the enemy's village and return to his own safely. The young chief seemed, however, to be just as great and nimble as he. When they came in sight of their band, the members who had been watching for them saw them running on the prairie. "Ho, ho!" they said, "White-Eagle-Feather is coming." Such was the shout. And it was White-Eagle-Feather behind the young chief.

The young chief slowed up then, and White-Eagle-Feather caught up with him. Now they were running side by side. They were in plain sight of their band, and White-Eagle-Feather said to the young chief, "This way we shall do is this: if I get in first, I shall call for my prize; then, when you get in, you can call for yours. That is the way we generally do here."

The young chief said, "I am going to get the first prize." And he ran as well as he could. The young chief got there first. The pipe was lighted and held up to him to smoke. He took only three or four puffs and called for the first prize. So they brought it to him, and put the wampum around him. Then White-Eagle-Feather entered.

After both had finished smoking, White-Eagle-Feather arose, and said, "I wish to tell you all something. As long as I have been with you, for these many years, I have been the only one who has been able to enter the village of the enemy. Whenever a man went along with me, he was killed, and I was the only one that returned. For that reason I always thought I was the bravest man. I have changed my mind now. This young man here has been made fun of because he was a stranger to us, but I say he is the bravest man among us, and I shall make friends with him."

125

How
the Two
Divisions
of the
Winnebagos
Came Together

Then the young chief arose, and said, "Friend, the great spirits above, on this earth, and below the earth, call me the Yankton. My name is not Prisoner-Man. White-Eagle-Feather wants to make friends with me and I am going to make friends with him."

Then they went home from the camp. It took six days to reach their village. They danced with their two scalps. Thus they danced all summer. After a while, the young chief married. White-Eagle-Feather also married. Both had sons. Both lived together in the same lodge. When enemies intended to come to the village, these two men in their dreams would have knowledge of it and make preparations to defend themselves.

Then the great spirits told this young chief to go home to his brother and sister, because the two of them, who were both younger than himself, were sick and pining for him. (He had been away from his people for many years.) He returned home with White-Eagle-Feather. When they got there in the night, the old man said, "Oh, my son!" But the old woman took a wooden poker and hit him with it, saying, "You have no son. You abused your own son and made him leave us for a long time. Whenever an enemy came, he knew it beforehand through his dreams. He was able to warn the people, and they were able to make preparations to meet the enemy."

He stayed with his people for four years, and after that he induced the two tribes to move together. From that time on, the members of White-Eagle-Feather's band formed part of the Winnebago Tribe. It was really the two parts of the Winnebago Tribe that had thus come together.*

*The Winnebagos had been at war with other tribes and various European nations since 1620. Their religious-social-political organization in the prereservation period was centered around warfare. Much violence appears in their stories.

The
Man Who
Visited the
Thunderbirds

By Joseph LaMere, Bear Clan

In the beginning, Earth-Maker [Ma-ona] created the world
and human beings, but the humans were so weak that they
were powerless to repel the attacks of the evil spirits
(*Wa'xopini ci'cik*) and the man-eaters, or giants (*Wan'geru'tege*).
These were invariably victorious over people until Earth-
Maker sent Hare [Wak'djin'ge'ga] to deliver the latter from
their enemies. After many hardships, Hare succeeded in
ridding the world of all the evil spirits that had molested it
for so long a time, and in conjunction with the Trickster,
Wak'djunk'aga, established the medicine lodge.

The story I shall tell you now is supposed to have taken
place in the time intervening between the sending out of
Trickster and Hare.

The giants had attacked a certain Winnebago village,
burned all the lodges, and killed and eaten all the inhabitants
with the exception of ten small boys and one little girl, whom
they wished to save until they had grown older. The children
thus felt alone, after they had dried their tears, they spent all
their time in fasting and hunting. As they grew older, all
they knew about themselves was that they were brothers and
sister. They knew nothing about their parents, nor about the
place they had come from. They had a long lodge with five
fireplaces and three entrances—one in the east, one in the
west, and one in the south.

Story collected by David Lee Smith.

The beds were so arranged around the fireplaces that the eldest brother slept directly opposite his sister.

This sister was treated with all imaginable love and consideration by all her brothers. They would not allow her to do any work. They themselves got the fuel, built the fire, cooked the food, washed, dressed, and combed her hair. As soon as these tasks were over, they would go out hunting and fasting.

One night when they were all in bed, it seemed to the eldest brother as though he heard someone talking to his sister. He kept awake all night, but was so shocked and thunderstruck that he could not utter a word. He listened again, and now there was no doubt that someone was talking to his sister, although he could not see him. He watched carefully to see if he could detect the person or discover him when he left the lodge. At break of day, however, in spite of his struggle to keep awake, he fell sound asleep, and when he woke up, the person had gone, and his sister was sleeping peacefully. He thought this rather peculiar, but said nothing to any of his brothers or to his sister.

He went hunting as usual in the morning, and on his return went to sleep. Again the same thing happened, and again just at daybreak he fell asleep. There seemed to him no doubt now that the man speaking to his sister had forced him to fall asleep just as he was leaving the lodge. The third and fourth nights the same thing was repeated, but at daybreak of the fifth day, to his surprise, he remained wide awake. He sat up and looked around to see if his brothers were all in their proper places. They were sleeping soundly and peacefully. Very much perplexed, he got up and, waking his brothers, he prepared everything as usual, and then went hunting.

It was generally their custom, when starting in the morning, to go together along a certain path for a time, and then to separate. This morning, however, just before they were to separate, the eldest called out to his brothers, "Let us stop here a little and smoke before we separate. We ought to do this oftener, so we can talk things over."

So they sat down, smoked, and chatted; then suddenly he rose and said, "Brothers, I have had a reason for asking you to stop and chat today. I am afraid something terrible has happened. During the last four nights a man has been talking to our sister. I myself heard him. For the first three nights I thought one of you was doing something disgraceful, but I was so choked with shame that I could not say anything to you about it. On the fifth morning, however, I heard him go out, and sitting up, I looked at all of your sleeping places, and took particular care to see if any of them was disordered or if any of you were disturbed in your sleep, but you were all sleeping quietly."

After he had finished speaking, the brothers discussed the incident, and finally came to the conclusion that the person who had appeared to their sister must have been some good spirit. They knew that such had happened before to other people, and in a way they felt glad that their sister had been selected, for they felt sure that it was no evil thing. They said nothing to her, preferring not to embarrass her, nor did they question her about what the eldest brother had heard. Thus things ran along for a few months without the brothers gaining any information. Finally, the sister came to them one day and told them that she was pregnant. They did not show the least surprise, but merely thanked her for the welcome information, and assured here that they were glad to know that they would soon have a new companion. They told her to take good care of herself and to do no work of any kind.

Months ran along in this way until the time came for her delivery. As soon as she told her brothers that she was about to be delivered of a child, they built her a little camp near their own, for in those times it was not customary for brothers to be present at the confinement of their sisters.* They supplied the lodge with a nice fireplace and provided

---

*In Winnebago culture, only the aunt of the birthing mother was allowed in her lodge when the mother was having her baby. It was taboo for the brothers to enter. After the baby was born, the mother and baby would move to the big lodge.

for her as best they could. When all was in readiness, she entered the new lodge. Some of her younger brothers were still working there, and not very long after her entrance a small iron cradle decorated in the most beautiful fashion was suddenly thrust in through the door. The brothers ran out immediately to thank the donor, but no one was to be seen. (As a matter of fact, it was the father of the child about to be born who had made the gift, but this the brothers did not know.)

After a short time the brothers left the lodge and the sister remained alone to be delivered of a boy. No sooner had the child been born that the ten brothers came in, congratulated her, and immediately proceeded to take care of their young nephew. So well did they do this, that soon nothing was left for her to do but to nurse him. The youngest brother detailed himself especially for the work of taking care of his little nephew, quitting hunting entirely, and staying home with him. Indeed, he seemed to love the little fellow more than did all the others.

Thus things went along until the baby could eat, though not talk. One night, the eldest brother was awakened, and sitting up in his bed again heard someone talking to his sister. No one could be seen, however, as on the former occasions. So now, despite his efforts, he fell asleep at daybreak. The second night the same was repeated, but on the morning of the fifth day he remained awake and he saw the person get up and walk out of the lodge followed by his sister, who took her sewing material with her.

When the brothers got up in the morning, they discussed the incident, but showed no surprise, because it did not seem strange to them that their sister should have followed her husband to his home, wherever that was. In the belief that such was the case, they went out hunting, as usual. However, when they returned in the evening and found out that their sister had not returned, they became worried, and the eldest one said, "I think we had better try to find out where she has gone." In the morning, he arose and went to seek her, the other brothers having gone hunting, as usual. When they returned in the evening, the eldest had not returned, and they resolved to send out the next one to look for him.

As the second did not return, they became very anxious, fearing something might have happened. So they said to one another, "Let us go in search of our sister." So the next morning the two next in age set out, not to return. Again two were sent out, and they did not return. Only four brothers were left now, and they finally decided to leave the youngest one home to take care of their little nephew, while they would start in search of the missing ones. They did not return.

Now only the youngest brother was left, and much as he desired to start in search of his brothers, the thought of this little nephew left alone unnerved him. "No," he said to himself, "it won't do for me to leave my nephew all alone. Surely something has happened to my brothers. Yes, I am going to see what has happened to them, and if I have to die—well, all right. I don't want to live alone."

Ever since his sister had left, the youngest brother had been feeding his nephew on deer brains. He would boil them and make a gruel out of them (this is supposed to be the most excellent food for an infant who has no mother to nurse him). The infant was still strapped to his cradle board. So, when finally the youngest brother prepared to go in search of his lost brothers, he placed the cradle board against the wall of the lodge and prepared some deer tail, which he boiled until it became soft. Then he freed the baby's arms so that they could move freely and suspended the deer skin from the top of the lodge in such a way that the infant could reach it whenever he wished. Then he started out.

He had proceeded only a little way when he heard his nephew crying, and losing heart he returned. "Don't cry, little nephew," he said, "for if Earth-Maker will let me, I will return soon." Then he started again and went a little farther. But he heard his nephew cry and returned. The third time he started he proceeded still farther, but again returned. The fourth time he started he ran, for he did not want to be tempted to return by hearing the cries of his nephew.

He took the trail of his brothers and followed it until he came to two camps—a small one and a large one. He entered the first one and found a very old woman sitting there. As soon as she saw him, she addressed him thus: "My poor grandchild, sit down here. I am very sorry for you." And then she went on to tell him what had happened to his sister and brothers. She told him that the person who had been talking to his sister the last time was a bad spirit, but that the sister had mistaken him for the father of her child and had accompanied him to this camp. However, he was not the father, as she afterwards found out.

All his brothers had been killed by this bad spirit, and she did not believe that he, the youngest, would escape their fate. The old woman then proceeded to tell him that his sister was by this time so completely under the influence of this bad spirit, that she was as bad as he, and preferred to help the spirit she now saw as her husband rather than her brother.

"Now, listen, my grandchild! The first thing that the bad spirit will ask you to do tonight will be to prepare a sweat bath for him; and in order to do that, he will tell you to fetch a certain stone. That stone belongs to him, and it is placed there for a certain purpose. Just as soon as you touch it, it will begin to roll down the hill, and you will roll with it. That is how some of your brothers met their death. Now, you just take a pole, walk up the opposite side of the hill, and touch it with the pole, and it will then roll down the hill. As soon as it has stopped rolling, you can pick it up and take it home.

"When you have brought this home, your brother-in-law will tell you to get the bark of a certain very large tree. That tree belongs to him and he keeps it there for a certain purpose. Just as soon as you touch the bark of the tree, the bark will fall on you and kill you. Some of your brothers met their death in that way. Now you take a stick and go as near as you can to the tree and throw the stick at it. It will hit the bark, which will fall off. Then just take as much of it as you want and bring it to him.

"When you have brought this, he will send you out again and tell you to fetch the lodge pole for the sweat house.

When you get to the place where he has sent you, you will find four large rattlesnakes lying curled up. These are what he meant you to get. Some of your brothers met their death there. They were killed by the snakes.

"So now, my grandson, take some tobacco along with you and give it to them, and ask them not to hurt you. Those snakes do not belong to him, but he is more powerful than they and he keeps them there as his slaves. He just gives them enough to eat and to drink. However, they have never had anything to smoke and they will be glad to accept your gift and not molest you.

"I shall put in my influence to help you with them, and then you will be able to take them with you. When you come to your bother-in-law's place, put their heads in the ground and twist their tails, and so you will have the finest of lodge structures. After this has been done, he will tell you to pick up the stone with your naked hand and carry it into the sweat house. Now, you know the stone belongs to him, and his purpose is to have it stick to your hand and burn you up. That is how some of your brothers met their fate. Now, my grandson, when it comes to that point, try to find some excuse to leave him, and come over to see me before you pick up the stone."

Shortly after the old woman had finished, the sister entered, and seeing her brother immediately addressed him, "Brother, I have brought you something to eat." Then she handed him a wooden bowl containing a large amount of liver as dry as a bone. He took the bowl, and as soon as he had noticed the contents, threw the bowl and liver straight into the face of his sister.

"I am not accustomed to eating this kind of food," he said. "My brothers, who brought me up, never gave me any food like this." His sister then left the lodge, and, it being suppertime, the old woman cooked him a supper of vegetables. After he had finished his supper, his sister came in again.

"Tenth-Son, your brother-in-law wants you to prepare his sweat bath. He is accustomed to using a certain stone that you will find yonder on the hill, and which he wishes you to get." Then she left the lodge. Her brother went to the hill and, following the advice of his grandmother, ascended it on the side opposite the stone, and touched it with his stick, and it rolled rapidly down the hill.

He then carried it to his brother-in-law's lodge, but left it outside. Then he went in to inform the brother-in-law that he had brought the stone. His brother-in-law merely nodded and told him to fetch the bark for the lodge structure. This he set out to do, and when he came near the tree, he carefully took a position of safety, and touched the bark with his stick. It fell with a terrific crash and he took as much as he needed and carried it to his brother-in-law. The latter merely nodded when it was brought and sent him to get the lodge poles.

When he came to the place where the snakes were confined, he took some tobacco and threw it to them. They accepted it and allowed him to seize them and carry them to his brother-in-law. When he arrived there he stuck their heads in the ground and twisted their tails, thus forming the poles of the sweat-bath lodge. Then he put the bark over these poles and the structure was complete.

As soon as everything was in readiness, his brother-in-law told him to place the stone in the lodge. Instead of doing this, however, he got up some excuse and went to see the old woman. She prepared for him some sacred sage and rubbed his hands and arms with it thoroughly and told him to return to the sweat lodge immediately and do as his brother-in-law had asked.* This he did, and much to the disgust of the latter the stone did not burn him in the least. Indeed, he got so provoked that he said to him ironically, "You think you are a clever fellow, don't you? I don't want to take a bath at all." And with this he went to sleep, and Tenth-Son returned to his grandmother,† with whom he stayed overnight.

---

*Sacred sage was always used in Winnebago sweat-lodge ceremonies. If a bad person attempted to use it, he would have bad luck.
† In Winnebago culture, all elderly women are "grandmother."

That night the old woman gave him further advice: "Grandson, you have done nobly, and I am very proud of you. But the hardest still remains to be done. Tomorrow your brother-in-law will ask you to go hunting with him, and he will take you out a considerable distance until he shall have killed a large buck deer, which he will ask you to pack with your bowstring so that the antlers of the deer are near your back. His intention is to have you run the antlers into your skull. If he does not succeed in that, he will step on the tail end of your moccasin to make you stumble and have the antlers break your back. Some of your brothers met their fate in that way." Then both fell asleep.

Early the next morning, his sister came and said, "Tenth-Son, your brother-in-law wants you to go hunting with him." So he went along with him, and after they had continued on their course for some time, the brother-in-law killed a big buck deer and told the boy to pack it. The boy knew what was going to happen, but nevertheless he said, "I have not got any pack string. How can I pack it?"

"Why, take your bowstring and do it. What is the matter with you, anyhow? Come, I will pack it for you," the brother-in-law answered angrily. So he untied the boy's bowstring and packed the deer for him. He doubled the deer up so that his antlers were quite near the boy's back. But the boy had been careful enough to secret a whetstone under the hair of his forehead, as his grandmother had instructed him to, so that the bowstring would touch the stone instead of his forehead.

When all was in readiness, they started home. The brother-in-law waited to see what would happen, but as the bowstring did not seem to cut the head of the young man, he proceeded to step on the tail of his moccasin. To his surprise the bowstring broke in two, causing the boy to stumble, but not injuring him, for the bowstring went one way and the pack the other. "What did you do that for?" the boy asked.

"Oh, just for fun," his brother-in-law answered. "I wanted to see what you would do." Then, much provoked, the bad spirit packed the deer with his own pack strap and walked home. The young boy returned to his grandmother.

The grandmother prepared the supper and said to him, "Grandson, you have done wonderfully well. You have fared far better than any of your brothers. But tomorrow will be a very hard day, and I don't know how I am going to help you. Your brother-in-law will ask you to go out hunting again and will send you to head off a deer. Then suddenly it will commence to snow severely, and before you are aware of it, you will be alone in the timber with no footprints to guide you. I shall not be able to help you then, but if you can think of anything that you obtained from the good spirits while fasting, or of any other way whereby you can protect yourself, do so tonight. That is all, my grandson."

In the morning, as usual, the sister came and said, "Tenth-Son, your brother-in-law wants you to go out hunting with him." So he accompanied him, and they went along until late in the afternoon. Suddenly a bear jumped out of the brush and, on seeing the hunters, ran away. The brother-in-law called the young boy and said, "Now you stay here while I take after him—and don't get frightened, because you can see my tracks right along."

As soon as he got out of sight, it began to snow and got very cold. The boy was not prepared for this and had no extra garment. He kept in the track of his brother-in-law as long as it was visible, but the fast-falling snow soon obliterated the last trace. He was lost. He stood there without moving for some time and then began to cry. He cried not so much for himself as for his little nephew, whom he pictured to himself left alone to starve. Suddenly he heard a voice near him. He wiped his tears away, and there in front of him stood a tall man.

"Tenth-Son, don't you know me?"

"No," answered the boy, "I never saw you before."

"Why, uncle," the person said, "I am the one whom you left in the cradle board when you ran away from me. Your brother-in-law is right over the hill yonder, skinning the bear. You go right over there now and you will see that he has a nice fire built for himself. He is cooking some meat. When you get there, just take the meat that he has cooked out of the fire and eat it yourself. He'll tell you to put it away, but don't pay any attention to him and go right on eating. Afterwards, he'll tell you to take the bear and pack it, and then you just tell him you won't do it. Let him do it himself.

"He will then threaten to kill you, but you just keep on refusing. Then he will get very angry and get ready to strike you. Just when he raises his club, call 'Wakan'djat'cora! Nephew, I'm about to be killed.' And I shall be there to help you."

So the young man did as he had been told and found his brother-in-law busy skinning and cooking the bear. He went straight to the fire and took the cooked meat out. "What are you doing there?" said the brother-in-law. "Put that back, and don't touch it again." The young man paid no attention to him. The brother-in-law said nothing for a while. Then he said, "Tenth-Son, pack the bear for me."

"I will not," answered the latter, "do it yourself."

"If you don't do it," retorted the former, "I shall kill you."

But the young fellow persisted in his refusal and this so enraged his brother-in-law that he lifted his club to strike him. Just as he was about to strike him, the boy cried out, "Wakan'djat'cora! Nephew, I'm about to be killed." Immediately there stood in front of him his nephew. The nephew then addressed the evil spirit.

"What are you trying to do to the boy?" he asked.

"Oh, nothing," the brother-in-law answered, "I was just fooling with him."

"Well, I'll fool with you too," the nephew said. And with that, he lifted his club and struck him on the head. It was like a thunder crash, and the evil spirit was smashed to pieces. There was nothing left of him. Then the nephew addressed his uncle. "I'll take the bear home for your grandmother." He thereupon packed the bear.

"Uncle," he continued, my mother has wronged you much, and although she was influenced, and compelled to do much of what she did, by the evil spirit, nevertheless you have a right to do with her what you will. I leave that to you entirely. If you think you have suffered so much pain and hardship that you ought to have your revenge, you may kill her."

"Well," answered the uncle, "I have indeed grieved very much, not so much for my brothers and myself as for you. And although I know she was influenced by the evil spirits, she must not live."

So they went home to the old woman. Then the uncle went to his sister's camp, killed her, and set the camp afire. They cut up the bear into chunks and gave it to the old woman. Then the uncle said, "Grandmother, I am going to leave you." And the grandmother said, "All right, grandson, I am going to leave you also. This is not my home. I just came up here to help you. My home is way down underneath the earth. The meat you gave me will last me almost as long as the world lasts, and all that I ask of you is to remember me occasionally by sacrificing some tobacco. I am the head spirit of the mice."

After she had departed, the nephew said, "Well, Uncle, now I'll have to leave you, too. I am going to my father. I came here only because my father asked me to."

But the uncle said, "Nephew, if you go away, I'll go along with you. You are not going to leave me here alone, are you?"

But the nephew replied, "Uncle, Earth-Maker does not permit us to take human beings to our homes, and I am sure my father would not like it. If you don't come along, I'll give you all kinds of supernatural powers. We can give greater supernatural powers for the warpath than any other spirits Earth-Maker has created. I'll also endow you with long life and allow you to give to your children as long of a life as you wish.

"I will also see that you have abundant game. You will only have to sit at your door to get all the game you desire, and as much wealth as you desire I will bestow on you. As Earth-Maker does not permit us to take human beings like yourself to our homes, you can see us only when we come on earth or when we appear to you in visions, when you are fasting."

But the uncle continued, "No, nephew, I am going along with you. I can't live without you." As the nephew saw it was of no avail, he said, "Step in my trail four times as you are about to start." The uncle stepped in his trail four times as he was about to start, and up they went.

They came to the western horizon. When they came near the home of the nephew, the uncle saw that the country was very similar to his own. They continued until they came to an oak timber. There they stopped. The nephew thereupon took his uncle between his palms and rubbed him, and he became smaller and smaller, until he was about the size of a Thunderbird egg. Then he placed him in a nest in the fork of one of the oak trees and said to him, "Uncle, stay here and be contented. Don't be uneasy. I shall come back to you in four days to see how you are getting along." He then went home to his father.

His father asked him, "Well, son, what have you been doing." He knew very well what his son had been doing, but he merely asked the question to see what answer he would get. The son answered, "Father, I have brought my uncle along with me."

"Well, where is he?"

"Over yonder in the tree. I'm going back to see him in four days."

"Well, son, it is not our custom to do what you have done, but as you have got him over here, I guess we will let it go."

After four days, the nephew went to see his uncle and found him with his bill sticking out of the egg, like a little chicken. "Uncle, you are doing fine; just be contented, and I will be back to see you in four days." When he came again, he found his uncle just hatched. "Uncle, you are doing fine; just be contented, and I will be back in four days." When he came again, the uncle was standing on the top of the tree, just over the nest—a full-grown, beautiful Thunderbird. "Ah, uncle, you look fine! Your feathers are far more beautiful, and you look far stronger than any of the rest of us." Thereupon the uncle jumped from the tree and found his bow and arrows lying on the ground ready for him. He picked them up and, together with his nephew, went to the home of Big-Hawk, the chief of the Thunderbirds.

There he stayed for a few days. One day he said to his nephew, "Let us go out, take a look at the country, and shoot pigeons." So he and his nephew went around shooting pigeons with a bow and arrow. They would stop to build a fire and cook their pigeons in the open. (The main food of the Thunderbirds at that time was snakes and all kinds of subterranean and aquatic animals.)

One day toward evening, the uncle, who was doing all the shooting, since his nephew used only a club, aimed at a pigeon. But the arrow missed aim and struck a spring where there was some white chalk. He went to get his arrow and painted himself with the chalk that had adhered to the point of the arrow. When he joined his nephew later, the latter saw the chalk on his face and said excitedly, "Where did you get that, uncle?"

"What do you mean?" asked the uncle.

"Why, what you have on your face. Those are the faces of the beaver, and big ones, too. You just give that to my father and tell him that he may use half of it for himself and give the other half to his people."

The uncle said, "You are speaking foolishly, nephew; I have not seen any beaver."

The nephew, however, replied, "Uncle, that is a beaver, and that is all there is to it."

"Well," answered the uncle, "you can tell your father whatever you want to, but I'm not going to give him something I have not seen." With that they started home, the nephew hurrying in order to inform his father of the great game they had discovered.

When they got home, the nephew told his father that his uncle had found a very large beaver and had given half of it to him and half to his people, to be used at a feast. The old man was delighted at this and in the morning took as many people as wanted to come along, roused the beaver out of his hole, killed him, and gave a great feast. From that time on, the uncle and his nephew went out to hunt beaver regularly, and each time they found more. They also discovered other animals—leeches, and different species of worms.

After the uncle had lived among the thunder-beings for a number of years, hunting with his bow and arrow, the chief of the thunder-beings decided to hold a secret meeting and discuss the advisability of keeping him among them. Big-Black-Hawk was also there. At that meeting it was decided that it would be impossible to keep the uncle with them forever. While he was unquestionably benefiting them very much, nevertheless it did not seem proper that an earthborn individual should live with thunder-beings. They did not decide upon any definite date, but they determined that he should not stay among them very much longer. When some of the younger Thunderbirds heard of this decision, they resolved to get rid of him as soon as possible.

Now, there was a very large water-spirit who inhabited a lake nearby. The lake's banks were so precipitous that the thunder-beings could never harm the spirit with their thunder and lightning. They would often go around to look at him, but they could never injure him.

The scheme of the young Thunderbirds was to entice the uncle to the lake, and while pretending to have him look at the water-spirit, push him in. So they told the nephew to come along with them, bringing his uncle. "Tell him", they said, "to take his bow and arrow along, for we are going to look at the water-spirit, and perhaps your uncle, who does such wonderful things, can devise some means of capturing the spirit."

So they all went to the lake, and while the uncle was looking at the water-spirit, they pushed him in. The bank was extremely steep, and he was immediately killed. Then they went home, leaving the nephew to weep for his lost uncle.

The nephew commenced mourning for him and walked around the lake for four years. One day while thus walking, he noticed a wing feather drifting toward the bank. He took it home with him, rubbed it between his palms, and transformed it into a Thunderbird egg. Then he put it in the fork of an oak tree and he said, "Uncle, I shall be back in four days." When he returned after four days, the bill was just sticking out of the egg. "That's all right, uncle, I shall be back in four days." When he came back, the egg was fully hatched. "It's all right, uncle, I shall be back in four days." At the end of the four days, the uncle was standing at the edge of the nest. "It's all right, uncle, I shall be back in four days."

In the meantime, the nephew had spoken to his father, Big-Black-Hawk, and he had said, "My son, we can't have that uncle of yours around here. You will have to take him back to the place where he came from. You may tell him that he may have anything he wants."

Then the nephew went to his uncle and found him perched on the top of the tree just over the nest, but he did not look as beautiful nor as strong as he did the first time. He looked like an ordinary Thunderbird. He came down to greet his nephew and they talked for a long time. The nephew told his uncle how he had mourned his death, but in spite of it all, his father would not allow him to stay with them.

"Earth-Maker would not like it," my father says, "for he would not want human beings to live together with the thunder-beings. Uncle, I have grieved long over what the thunder-beings did to you, and I am now going to take my revenge by telling you something. My father says that he will give you any one of the war clubs that we possess. When you enter the lodge, you will see a large number of them hanging along the walls of the lodge. Some look much better than others, but there will be one right next to the door that looks the shabbiest of them all. Take that one, and then you will make them weep, just as they made me weep."

Then they went home, and Big-Black-Hawk told the uncle that he must return to earth, but that he would give him any of the clubs that he saw suspended in the lodge.

The uncle got up, walked around the lodge, and examined the clubs one after another. When he got near the door, he turned around and said, "I thank you all for giving me this club, the worst of them all, for I don't want to take the best one that you have. I shall be perfectly satisfied with this shabby one." He took it, and just as his nephew had said, all the thunder-beings hung their heads and wept.

In the center of the lodge there was a little bowl filled with some liquid. Big-Black-Hawk got up and presented it to the uncle and told him to drink. As he drank, he seemed to hear the voices of millions of people begging for their lives. What he drank was really the brains of all the people that he was going to kill on the warpath. "What happened while you were drinking," Big-Black-Hawk said to him, "is a vision of what that club that you took is going to do for you."

Then the nephew took his uncle and, rubbing him between his palms, transformed him into human shape again. Then he accompanied him back to earth. He said to him, "Uncle, you may see me whenever you want to," and he bade him good-bye and left him.

The uncle joined a tribe of Indians and immediately began to go on the warpath, and by virtue of his wonderful club he was able to kill as many persons as he wanted.

After he had gone on doing this for several years, the thunder-beings held another council and Big-Black-Hawk said, "This will never do. If that man keeps on, he will soon destroy all the people on the earth. That club must be taken away from him."

So he sent his son down to tell his uncle that his club would have to be changed. The nephew came to the earth and told his uncle that he would have to take his club away from him, but that he would substitute one in its place that would do him excellent service. The uncle was very displeased to hear this.

Then the nephew called a meeting of all the different spirits of the earth. He had his uncle make a club exactly like the one that was to be taken away. He also told him to make a whistle. If ever he was on the warpath, and would blow that whistle, it would be the same as the voice of a Thunderbird, and they would send him their powers. The club, too, would possess great powers, although it would not possess the magical power of the first club.

Then the spirits who were assembled in council said, "We will endow him with our special powers." The snake gave him the power of concealing himself. The carnivorous birds gave the power of telling where the enemy was, and of seeing them in the nighttime. "In return for this, we shall eat the flesh of the people you kill," they said.

The spirits underneath the earth said, "We shall give you a medicine. If you paint yourself with it, you will have more strength than your enemies. You will be able to outrun them. If they follow you and get your scent, this will overpower them, and they will not be able to go any farther." Then the nephew returned to his home. The war club and the powers bestowed on the uncle were handed down from one generation to another, always remaining in a certain clan.

Thus things went on until the Indians came in contact with the whites. They saw the steel points of the whites and thought the club would look better if it contained these points. This they decided to do after a great meeting and feast had been held.

The
Orphan Boy
Who Was Captured
by the Bad Thunderbirds

By Joseph LaMere, Bear Clan

In a little village there lived an orphan boy and his grandmother. As the boy grew up, he found a friend of the same
age. One day they went out to get some hickory wood to
make bird arrows. When these arrows were ready, the
orphan boy went out hawk hunting. He captured a young
pigeon hawk. He became fond of it and kept it at home as
a pet.

One day, he put some tobacco in a little bundle and tied
it around the hawk's neck. Soon after this the pigeon hawk
disappeared, but it returned not long after, without the
tobacco bundle. So he put another bundle around its neck
and soon the bird again disappeared. This incident was
repeated again and again.

One day long after, when the hawk was full grown, the boy
again tied a bundle of tobacco around its neck and told the
bird that he thanked it that it had stayed with him so long,
but now that it was full grown, if it cared to, it could go
wherever it wished. Thereupon the bird flew away and never
returned.

The two friends, one day, went out again to find some
dogwood for pointed arrows. They went around the brush
and accidentally were separated, for it was a cloudy and
rainy day. While they were separated, the bad thunder-
spirits seized the orphan and carried him to their home.

Story collected by David Lee Smith.

The friend hunted for him a long time, but then gave up in despair and returned home. The friend returned day after day to the place where his friend had disappeared, to search for him and to mourn for him.

When the bad spirits seized the orphan, they tied him to the floor, binding his wrists and feet to stakes. Their purpose was to hold him in this position until there was nothing left in his stomach, because it was their rule that only then would they devour human beings.

While the boy was thus extended, they watched him carefully in order to prevent his escape.

One day the little pigeon hawk thought he would go to see this person of whom the thunder-spirits were talking so much. What was his surprise to recognize in the prisoner the man who had given him all the tobacco, and with whom he had lived for so long a time!

He went out and killed some pigeons, roasted them, and put some bones and some of the meat under his wings and went back to see the prisoner. He managed as best he could to drop some meat into his mouth. He kept on doing this every day until the bad thunder-spirits began to mistrust him. "This man," they said to themselves, "ought to be cleaned out by this time, and if he is not, that pigeon hawk must be feeding him secretly." So the next time the hawk appeared, they decided to put him out. One of them took hold of him and pushed him toward the door. The pigeon hawk, however, intentionally fell into the fire, burned himself badly, and crying at the top of his voice ran to his brother, Big-Black-Hawk, the chief of the Thunderbirds. "What is the matter, brother?" the latter asked. So Pigeon-Hawk told his brother the whole story as piteously as he could—of how the man who was now starving had befriended him on earth and given him much tobacco, and how he was now a prisoner and about to be devoured.

Big-Black-Hawk got angry and went over to the place where the prisoner lay and told the spirits that they had done wrong in bringing this man up there to be eaten; that he had tried to be patient, and had not reprimanded them. When, however, they pushed one of their comrades into the fire, he could no longer be quiet. They could not have their prisoner. So he cut the prisoner loose and took him along with him.

Little-Pigeon-Hawk, in the meantime, brought him pigeons. He roasted them and fed him for he was almost starved to death. After the prisoner put on weight again, he made a bow and some arrows for himself and went out hunting with Little-Pigeon-Hawk.

After a while he found some beavers and grizzly bears. The first beaver was found by accident, an arrow falling into a well and getting smeared with chalk. When the orphan found the spirits were anxious to have these beavers and grizzly bears, he went out hunting for them regularly. Now these animals had been there all the time, but being spirits themselves, like the thunder-spirits, they possessed the power of hiding themselves from the Winnebago boys, although this did not protect them from the boys' weapons.

After a while, Big-Black-Hawk told his younger brother that he would have to bring his human friend back to the earth. "It is not that I don't like him," Big-Black-Hawk said, "but he does not belong here, and Earth-Maker would not approve of it." So Big-Black-Hawk told the orphan that he had benefited the thunder-spirits very much, but that he could not remain with them and would have to return to his home. He gave him a club; however, he was to make a substitute of the club before he went back to earth. Pigeon-Hawk took him back and when he arrived on the earth, the orphan made a club and returned the original to Pigeon-Hawk.

The next evening, his old friend came to the brush as usual and was very surprised to find him there. The orphan told his friend to go home and order some young, unmarried people to build a lodge and have it scented with white cedar leaves.

The friend did as he was bidden, and after that he and the orphan, armed with his club, went to the lodge and told the young, unmarried people to go out hunting and bring a large buck, for they wanted to make a feast. The orphan

147

The
Orphan Boy
Captured
by Bad
Thunderbirds

assured the people that they would have no difficulty in finding one: they had but to go across the hill.

They did as they were bidden and came home with a large buck. Then he told them to invite to the feast as many people as they wished. The next day, and when all were assembled in the lodge, the orphan told the people to get two more deer for the next day's feast. The next day he told them the same. On the fourth day he told them to get four big bears. On this day he told them that he and his friend were going to walk around the country the next day, and if any young men wished to come along, they might.

They all understood what he meant—that he was going on the warpath. So a good many decided to go along. They traveled that day until noon. Then the orphan told a few of his companions to go a little way and kill some animals. At suppertime, he told them the same. After supper, he told his companions that he was going to attack a certain camp. The spirit-birds and other animals were helping and directing him, so he knew he would have no difficulty in finding the camp he was in search of.

When all was ready, they started out and killed all the inhabitants of the camp. They kept on going from camp to camp, killing all the inhabitants. After they had killed the inhabitants of the fourth camp, the orphan told his friends that he was going to stop and would thereafter go on the warpath only in order either to revenge someone or attack an enemy.*

*As noted in an earlier story, warfare was relevant in the Great Lakes area at the time of contact and this violence always found its way into Winnebago stories. It is not that the Winnebagos wanted to fight; they had to, to protect their families and loved ones. Stories like these are always told by Winnebago veterans, because they teach the younger generation to protect their families from harm. That is why many young men and women join the armed forces today.

Legend

By Keely Bassette, Water Spirit Clan

One day, Ma-ona looked down at this earth he had created and noticed that it was very smooth and his people were slipping all over the place because they couldn't keep their balance. He felt so badly about this that he began to cry, and when he did, big teardrops fell from his eyes onto the earth below. When the first drop hit, the earth began to shake. Then another drop landed and things really began to move. Great tracts of land were forced up, creating enormous craters. Tall mountains soon arose.

Eventually, Ma-ona noticed that his tears were creating oceans and rivers and lakes. Because of the weight of these features, the earth moved and shifted and the people could move about and not be afraid of sliding all over the place.

That is how the earth became uneven and how mountains and oceans were created.

The
Legend
of the Bear Clan

A modern legend by Joi St. Cyr, Bear Clan

Back in the days before the people and the animals spoke different languages, they had the ability to understand each other.

A young boy became separated from his people on their trip to their winter home during an early snowstorm. The young boy couldn't find his way, but instead found a cave, into which he crawled. In this cave, there lived a large black bear who had just begun his winter sleep.

The bear became very angry when disturbed by this boy and asked him why he would invade his home without permission. The young man was raised by respectful parents and replied to the bear, "I am lost, cold, and hungry."

The bear, seeing this pitiful sight, allowed his kind heart to rule his reply. He answered the boy with a loud growl, "You tell me why I should help you, when you would make a fine winter feast."

The young boy was sharp and he told the bear that he would very much like to learn the wisdom and knowledge the bear possessed. Through his flattery, the boy induced the bear to allow him to stay in his cave.

The winter passed quickly. As we all know, bears sleep during this time, and the bear awoke only to hunt.

By the time spring returned, the boy and the bear were inseparable friends. The bear showed the young man his powers and why and how he came to be. The boy taught his hunting skills and the bear allowed him to use the bear's magical powers of healing and traveling with his mind.

The bear possessed the magical healing and power of his mind because, even with all his physical attributes of strength and largeness he was too big to travel quickly. This is why the creator endowed him with such powers. The young man realized this and therefore wanted these powers to assist him to find his people and share the healing powers. The bear was aware of this and allowed the boy to use the powers for good purposes only. The bear helped him to find his people. The boy also was prohibited from harming his brother or taking him for food.

Soon, two springs had passed and the air again began to smell of summer. Finally, it was time for the boy to return to his people. The young man thanked his friend. He told the bear that he wished to take his powers and symbols back to his people for all to share. That is why almost all Native Americans have a Bear Clan in their tribe.

Ma-ona,
the Thunder-beings,
and the Young Hunter

By David Lee Smith, Thunder Clan

When the Winnebagos still roamed the forests of the Great Lakes country, there once lived an old grandfather and his young grandson. When the boy was first born, he was bestowed with a name of the Thunder Clan. His grandfather named him Thunder-Hunter.

As the boy grew older, the thunder-beings gave him special powers to be a great and powerful hunter. For many seasons, while he was growing into manhood, the young grandson hunted for his people. Everything he shot, he gave away. He gained a lot of respect among his elders, for none of them were ever hungry. That was until the grandson reached his thirteenth year.

In that year, something came over the young grandson. One day, while out hunting with others his own age-group, he became cocky and arrogant. He made fun of them because none of them could shoot any game. And when he brought his kill home, he would not share with anyone. After eating his dinner, he went to bed without even thanking the thunder-beings for his power. The grandfather knew something was the matter, but did not say anything.

Early the next morning, the grandson went out hunting again. But this time, he returned home with nothing. He told his grandfather that all the animals were scared of him. "Tomorrow, I will hunt ducks," he said. "for it is the season that the ducks fly south." After eating his supper, the young grandson went to bed. The old grandfather only looked at him with tears in his eyes, because the grandfather knew what was the matter. But he kept his mouth shut. It was the thunder-beings who gave the young hunter his powers, not he.

The next day, and for ten days after, the grandson went hunting and returned with nothing. He told his grandfather, "I know what is the matter. I need to fast." So he laid on his right side and fasted for ten days. Then he turned on his left side and fasted for ten more days. After he did this, the grandson arose and went hunting, without even praying for the thunder-beings' help.

When the grandson approached a small lake, he lay in hiding and waited for the ducks. When the sun was risen in the east, he saw some ducks flying toward him from the north. "This time the ducks are mine," he said to his bow and arrow. "Fly straight and true." When the ducks passed overhead, he drew his arrow back and shot. And as before, the arrow fell to the ground.

When the evening star was lighting up the western sky, the grandson approached his grandfather's lodge and went to bed without even eating. For the young grandson felt very bad and alone.

When the young hunter finally went to sleep, the thunder-beings called his spirit into the heavens. He found himself standing in front of Ma-ona, the Creator, and his helpers the thunder-beings. Ma-ona said, "Years ago when you were born, I told the thunder-beings to give you powers to make you a great hunter." After a few moments, Ma-ona continued, "Over the years, you did a good job with your powers. No one in your village was ever hungry, until lately." Ma-ona approached the young hunter closer and stared him in the eyes and finally said, "I told the thunder-beings to take away your powers because you became too conceited. That is why you could not shoot anything." The young hunter finally understood what happened to him.

153

Ma-ona,
the Thunder-
beings,
and the
Young Hunter

After a few moments, Ma-ona turned and walked away. The thunder-beings said in one voice, "Ma-ona told us to give back your powers, but never again brag on yourself. Only hunt for the food for the village."

When those last words were spoken, the young hunter woke up. He sat up and saw his grandfather preparing him breakfast. "Good morning my grandson," the grandfather said in a happy voice. "Are you going hunting, today?" His grandson smiled and said, "Yes, my grandfather, I shall go hunt for the people."

So the young hunter did learn his lesson and never again was he conceited. As the years went by, he became an even better hunter than before, and regained the respect that he had lost among his people.

The
Legend
of Ho-poe-kaw

By David Lee Smith, Thunder Clan

One of the greatest of Winnebago chiefs was not a man but a woman. Her name is still spoken whenever contemporary Winnebagos talk about political leadership. It has been more than two hundred years since the passing of Ho-poe-kaw, but the legend lives on.

They said it was during the month of the Digging Moon (May) when Ho-poe-kaw was born. She was the only child of the last true chief of the Winnebago people. On a clear, bright, sunny morning, she was presented to her people. To the Winnebago people it was an omen—an omen of good after suffering all spring with thunderstorms. It was also a time of great war, when the Winnebago joined their ally the Mesquakie Indians against the hated French.* Ho-poe-kaw's father was of the Thunder Clan and her mother was of the Eagle Clan.

As the years went by, young Ho-poe-kaw was taught the Winnebago way by her mother's sisters and her mother's brothers. Then one stormy night, she was called to her father's lodge. The old chief had passed away in his sleep. The entire tribe went into mourning, and the Grand National Council of the twelve clans debated on the issue of succession. Ho-poe-kaw found peace in the forest among her friends the animals. As a young girl of eighteen, she was

*The Fox Wars, 1703–1716 and 1722–1737.

unprepared for what lay in store for her. But the spirits of the dead chiefs were with her and they made a pact with the thunder-beings that she would be the greatest chief of all of them.

During the closing of the Corn Popping Moon (August), the council elected her first chieftainess of the Winnebago people. Half of the tribe left for the Mississippi, because a woman chief was unheard of in that day and age.

At the age of nineteen, she became an ally of the French people, who named her Glory-of-the-Morning, a translation of Ho-poe-kaw. In the first week of the Elk-Calling Moon (September), she was wed to a French military officer and, out of that union, would arise the famous DeCorah family.

In the cool days of the Deer-Digging Moon (October), young Ho-poe-kaw and her war chiefs were invited to a council with the Upper Great Lakes tribes. After the council, they fell upon a Mesquakie hunting party and sent every one of the enemy to the spirit world. Ho-poe-kaw was finally caught at Little Butte des Morts Lake, and she almost went to the Spiritland herself. It was said the thunder-beings intervened and turned the tables on the Mesquakie. The Mesquakies were caught at Starved Rock, Illinois, and almost terminated to the last man.

Ho-poe-kaw felt sorry for her people's former allies, and she pleaded with other tribes on their behalf to the French. Much to the displeasure of the French, they granted Ho-poe-kaw's request. Peace finally came to the Winnebagos and the smile was once more on the face of Glory-of-the-Morning, who had just turned twenty-six years of age.

The smile on Ho-poe-kaw's face seemed to vanish overnight. Her husband for the last seven years left her and returned to Quebec with his daughter Oakleaf. But deep in her heart, Ho-poe-kaw knew the thunder-beings were putting her to a test—a test she would pass with flying colors. With a man out of her life, she devoted herself fully to the warpath. In 1752, under her orders, Winnebago warriors attacked their age-old enemies the Michigamia and the

Cahokians. In 1755, Ho-poe-kaw sided with the French in the great war for the empire.

Under her eldest son's leadership, the Winnebago joined other Great Lakes tribes and attacked the British at Pickawellany and destroyed Edward Braddock on his way to Fort Duquesne. Then during the month of the Deer-Mating Moon (November), Ho-poe-kaw's warriors raided into Pennsylvania, Maryland, Virginia, Kentucky, and Tennessee. In all her victories, Ho-poe-kaw never fully forgot her one true love. Then came the tragedy at Quebec, when the only man in her life was killed while fighting alongside their son Chou-ke-ka. The year was 1759 and Ho-poe-kaw had just turned forty-eight years of age.

In 1763, something seemed to come over Ho-poe-kaw. She seemed to be withdrawn and tired. When Pontiac went to war with the Long-Knives, she declined. Day after day, Ho-poe-kaw went into the forest and prayed for her people, and the thunder-beings were kind, for they brought peace to the Winnebagos again. The legends say that one day, while walking through the pine trees, Ho-poe-kaw heard an owl calling her name. She knew it was an omen of death. Ho-poe-kaw was both sad and proud for what she had done for her people. Sad, because so many of them died in fighting for their land, and proud, that her sons would carry on the fight for her. One night in the Deer Antler-Shedding Moon (December), Ho-poe-kaw had a vision from her father. He was calling her name.

The snow was falling heavily when daylight broke and the stillness of the morning was shattered by the rumblings of thunder. This was odd, since the fall storms had passed two months before. Ho-poe-kaw's sons ran quickly to her lodge, and when they got there they found Ho-poe-kaw dead. The chief lay wrapped in her furs with a smile playing on her lips. Ma-ona, the Creator, had called her home.

The legend of Ho-poe-kaw will never die as long as there are Winnebagos left in the world. And when the last Winnebago passes on, Ho-poe-kaw will walk with that person as they both enter the Spiritland of the Creator forever.

How
Gray-Wolf Became
Guardian of the World

By David Lee Smith, Thunder Clan

At the time of Creation, Ma-ona made four brothers, Green-Wolf, Black-Wolf, White-Wolf, and Gray-Wolf. These four brothers at first roamed the surface of the world, but three brothers went beneath the earth, and are still there, appearing to Wolf Clan people occasionally. Gray-Wolf is the only one that is seen above the ground.

Ma-ona named the green wolf Kera-co-ra. This wolf was in charge of the day. The second wolf that Ma-ona created was the black wolf, who was in charge of the night. His name was Shunk-cank-sep-ka. The third wolf carried the name of Shunk-cank-ska, or White-Wolf. This wolf was in charge of all things sacred. The last wolf that Ma-ona created was Hin-rhoc-ka, the gray-haired wolf. His duty was the protection of mankind. This is the legend of the four wolves.

There was once an old man who lived all alone except for the company of four dogs. These dogs kept him company and supplied him with friendship in his elder years.

One day, while out picking berries, the old man fell and broke his ankle. As the days went by, he became so hungry that he started to eat his bear rugs because he could not hunt for his food. This brought some concern to the dogs. One night, while the old man slept, the dogs held council. The first dog said, "We should go hunt for our master, for he is very hungry." The second dog cut in and said, "No! No! He was always unkind to us and treated us like dogs." This brought a laugh from the third dog, "Ha ha, we are dogs you fool, that is why Ma-ona created us with four legs and a tail." After the laughter died down, the fourth dog said, "Our brother is right, it is our duty to hunt for our master, for he has kept us with him through all our young years." So it was agreed on that they would go hunting the next morning.

At daybreak, all four dogs left, but first dog was the only one who came back with food. The old man blessed him and called him Kera-co-ra, and gave him powers to hunt during the day. Not to be outdone, the second dog left during the night and brought back to the old man some food by morning time. So the second dog was blessed by its master and named Shunk-cank-sep-ka. He was given powers to hunt during the night.

The third dog saw what his master had done to his brothers, and he decided to outdo both of them. With sacred herb and the wood of the cedar tree, the third dog eased the old man's pain and fixed his leg. The master was very pleased and made him in charge of everything that is sacred. He named the third dog, Shunk-cank-ska.

The only dog that wasn't given any power was the fourth dog, and all his brothers looked down on him because of this. One day, while out hunting for himself, the fourth dog spotted a large war party coming. He knew his brothers could not help him because first dog was out hunting, second dog was sleeping, and third dog was praying. Therefore, fourth dog attacked the war party himself.

All day the battle raged, and at sundown the enemy retreated. The fourth dog went back to his master's lodge to lick his wounds. Seeing that he was hurt, the master said, "Anything wrong?" The fourth dog said, "No master, for I am going to sleep." The next day, the fourth dog again left and battled the war party. And for the next two days after, he did the same thing. At the end of the fourth day, the enemy was all killed. All this fighting brought a change over Fourth-Dog. He became wild and mean.

The master, finally seeing what he did, said, "Fourth-Dog, from this day forward, I will give you special powers

159

How
Gray-Wolf
Became
Guardian
of the World

to hunt both day and night, and powers to be unafraid of anything." After blessing him, the master said, "Your job now is to run the wilds, for I am going home to Ma-ona, and you will be the protector of mankind from this day forward." As a parting gesture, the old master placed Fourth-Dog's brothers beneath the earth. They would become protectors of the underworld.

From time to time, humans call on White-Wolf, who always brings them good luck. Hunters call on Green-Wolf, who brings them good luck hunting during the day. The night people call on Black-Wolf, who guards their camp during the night. But Gray-Wolf is free, and his call is always heard the world over, for he is the mightiest wolf of them all. He is the protector of the human race.

The
Evening Star

By David Lee Smith, Thunder Clan

Thousands upon thousands of seasons ago, when the Winnebagos were still in the lake country, there lived a powerful shaman. This shaman was once known far and wide for his power, and all people, enemy and friend alike, respected him.

At first he used his power only for the good of the people. Then he fell in love with the chief's daughter, who was the prettiest young woman of the tribe. The trouble was that the chief's daughter did not like the shaman. He tried everything to please her. He bought her honey, furs, and flowers, but nothing he did could change her opinion of him. So the shaman resorted to the thing he never used before, and that was evil magic.

The shaman knew, that if he used it, the evil magic would turn against him, but he was deeply in love. Nothing else mattered to him except the chief's daughter. So one dark night he called upon the evil spirits, who gave him a bag of love medicine to use on the chief's daughter. He then laid his plans very carefully, so no one would become suspicious of him. He planned to use the evil magic at the dance of the summer solstice.

The chief's daughter had plans of her own. She fell in love with a young warrior of the nearby Beaver Tribe. This tribe was reputed to be large and strong. The daughter's father, who was the chief, welcomed the idea of the mating, for in the process they would gain a strong ally. So, little known to the shaman, the marriage was to be consummated on the summer solstice.

As the day approached, the shaman was ordered to prepare a ritual drink for the marriage. When he found out who was getting married, he about fell over dead. He had worked hard and was not about to lose the chief's daughter to someone else.

That night, as the village lay sleeping, he turned himself into an owl and flew to the chief's lodge. Once there, he sprinkled dust over the sleeping form of the daughter, and before anyone awakened, he returned to his own lodge. The next day, the celebration would start at sunrise, so he went to sleep with an evil smile on his lips.

The next morning, after the sun appeared on the eastern horizon, the brave young warrior of the Beaver Tribe appeared with his people. The chief ordered his daughter to get ready and sent word to the shaman to bring the ritual drink. The shaman arrived when the marriage ceremony was just about over. The ritual drink that he brought would be the final act to the marriage vows. When the daughter saw the shaman, her mind seemed to snap, and she fell in love with the shaman. The evil magic that the shaman used had done its purpose. When the chief asked his daughter to give the ritual drink to her new husband, she gave it to the shaman, and the marriage was done.

Both the chief and the Beaver warrior stood there aghast. Then both men flew into a rage. The warrior promised that war would be arranged, for no one would make a fool out of him. The chief answered that his people would be waiting. After the Beaver party left, the chief ordered his daughter and the shaman from the village. He loved his daughter dearly, but he could not break up the marriage. That would go against tribal tradition.

As the months passed, the chief's daughter became pregnant for the shaman. At the night of the birth, the daughter died after giving birth to a little deformed girl. The shaman now knew that his own evil magic had turned against him. The shaman was very heartbroken, but he buried his wife, took his daughter, and moved still further from his old village than before.

As the years went by, the old shaman used what good powers he had left to raise his daughter right. She became a mighty hunter and a powerful warrior. The only thing she lacked was her own people. The old shaman knew that her own people would never want her because she was deformed somewhat in the face. So his young daughter stayed with him until he died.

After the daughter laid her father to rest, she had a vision from her dead mother. Her mother appeared to her in a dream. "My daughter," she said, "forgive your father for what I am about to tell you. Long ago, your father used love medicine on me and won me away from my true husband-to-be. Now his tribe and our tribe are still fighting an endless war, and they need your help." The mother touched her daughter's hand and continued, "My father, the chief, is very old, but tell him I am sorry for what has happened. I hope in his heart he can forgive me." Tears seemed to flow from her mother's eyes. "Now go my daughter, and help your people, for the last battle is about to start, and remember I love you always." As the vision faded, the mother said, "Follow the river to its mouth; there you will find your people." With that, the mother vanished and the daughter woke up.

In her hand she saw a small, red stone hanging on a string. She had seen it once before, hanging from her mother's neck, so she knew her dream was more than a dream. The red stone was her mother's personal medicine, given to her by her father the chief. Quickly she gathered her weapons and proceeded south, following the raging river.

Days later, she approached the mouth of the river. On the opposite bank she saw a large village, and she knew she had found her people. She then climbed the tallest pine and looked far to the west. There she saw smoke rising from four camps, with hundreds of men forming ranks. "So there's the enemy," she said aloud. "I better help my people, for they are outnumbered and will suffer greatly." Then she climbed down the tree and prepared herself a sweat lodge. If she was going to fight, she had to purify herself, as her father the shaman told her to.

During the night, as the stars came out, she prepared her own medicine, for she was not the shaman's daughter for nothing. She knew she had to cross to her people's village in order to approach the enemy. She did not want them to know that she was fighting for them, because her mother was the cause of the war and she did not know how her people would react. So when the clouds darkened the night, she changed herself into a small owl and flew over her people's village.

About the same time she was turning into an owl, her grandfather, the chief, came out of his lodge to pray to Maona for victory the following day. He was tired, and growing older each day. His thoughts kept going back to the scene eighteen years ago, when he exiled his daughter from his village. Now he was ready for death, and his only hope was that the Creator would forgive him for what he had done. Just then he looked up to the heavens and seemed to see an owl passing though the broken clouds. "An omen," he said to himself. "An omen of death, but whose death?" he said quietly. (An owl is an evil omen in Winnebago beliefs.)*

At sunrise the next day, the chief gathered his warriors and marched out to meet the enemy. There was no enemy, for all the enemy were dead. In the middle of the dead Beaver warriors, he spotted a young girl in tribal dress, dying from many mortal wounds. Then he saw around her neck a small, pretty, red stone, hanging on a string. Tears formed in his eyes as he knelt down and cradled the girl's head in his arms. She slowly opened her eyes and said, "Grandfather, please forgive my mother and my father, and please take me home to our people." The grandfather grabbed his granddaughter in his arms and with his warriors marched back to the village.

*In Winnebago culture, the hooting of an owl is an omen of bad luck. The Winnebagos believe that owls are really bad spirits who want Winnebago souls. Many Winnebagos offered them tobacco to appease them.

Just as the sun was going down, the chief's granddaughter died. The whole village went into mourning. Then a strange thing happened. The dead girl was lifted into the heavens by the four spirit-winds. For Ma-ona himself felt very bad, and he wasn't about to let the little girl die after saving his own people. So as the sun disappeared, Ma-ona placed the chief's daughter in the evening sky. She became the evening star. Now she guards the people forever. If you ever look real hard, people say you can see the star shine brightly as if it is smiling. Smiling that she is now home with her people.

Little-Sister
Brings Darkness
over the Earth

By David Lee Smith, Thunder Clan

At the beginning of time, it was the animals who ruled the earth and it was the humans who were the hunted. After raiding one particular village for some time, the animals wiped out the human population, except for an old grandmother and her little granddaughter. One day the granddaughter's brother paid them a visit. After feeding her grandson, the grandmother said to him, "Every day when I go out to pick plants for our meals, I see the animals getting closer to our little village, and I am scared for your little sister."

Her grandson spoke, "That is why I am here grandmother, I brought little sister a bow and arrows." After giving the bow and arrows to his little sister, he continued, "I have to go home now to watch my other little sisters, so please take care." After saying good-bye to both of them, he left. Both the grandmother and her granddaughter watched the young man until he was out of sight. Grandmother said, "We better go to bed now, because I have to get up early to go hunt berries." So both went to bed just as the stars came out.

The next morning before going out, the grandmother said to the little sister, "Don't ever leave this village, and use your bow and arrows only on little birds, because the bow is too small for the big animals."

After grandmother left, Little-Sister played around the village until she heard a bluebird making noise. She hid behind a tree until the bluebird came in sight. Then before the bluebird could fly away, Little-Sister shot him. When grandmother came home she showed her the bluebird. "What should I do with all the pretty feathers, my granddaughter," she said. "Shall I make a blanket?" Her granddaughter said excitedly, "No! No! grandmother, make me a cloak." So the grandmother made her the prettiest cloak in the world.

167

Little-Sister
Brings
Darkness
over the
Earth

The next day, grandmother again went out berry picking, leaving the little sister at home alone. She was given strict orders not to leave the village. But the little sister wanted to show off her beautiful cloak, so against her grandmother's wishes, she went out for a walk. After walking for many miles, Little-Sister decided to take a nap and rest. When she awoke, the sun was directly overhead, and she saw that she was surrounded by many animals.

Little-Sister tried to move and saw that she could not because the sun had shrunk her cloak when she was asleep. The animals, seeing her predicament, started laughing at her. Little-Sister became terrified, and struggled all the more, until she ripped her cloak in half and the pretty bluebird feathers flew all over the place. In this commotion, the little sister fled. She ran as fast as her little legs could carry her. Just as the sun was going down, she made it home.

She turned and shouted both at the sun and the animals, "Both of you shall pay for ruining my beautiful cloak, and don't think you're so mighty and far away that I can't get even with you." With that, she fell to her knees and cried. Grandmother picked her up and carried her into the lodge. When the stars came out, both the grandmother and Little-Sister worked on a plan.

The next morning, Little-Sister went out and climbed the tallest tree she could find. When the sun was straight up, she shouted down to the animals, "Today is the day—you shall be paid for ruining my cloak. Both you and the sun shall pay." Arrow after arrow she shot into the sun, until the sun started to disappear. For little known to the animals, Little-Sister's grandmother, the moon, was covering up the sun.

When the last arrow was shot, the sun disappeared. Darkness came over the land and day became night. Now it was the animals who became terrified. "What shall we do?" one of them asked. "We shall all die," another one explained. "Someone go tell Little-Sister to bring back the sun, for the plants are dying and we shall have nothing to eat," said the mighty bear.

Out of the darkness a tiny voice said, "I will climb the tree and ask Little-Sister to bring back the light." So a small tree mouse climbed and climbed, while below him the animals stood very still. The only sound in the world was their heavy breathing. Finally, a small speck of light showed in the heavens. Then with the passing of time, more and more light started shining, until the sun escaped the moon and was once again shining in the heavens.

The animals now knew that Little-Sister was smarter than them. So they made a pact with her. If she kept the sun shining, they would become the hunted and she and all humans would become the hunter. To see that they kept their word, Grandmother-Moon stayed in the heavens. And to this day, the animals have kept their word.

Ha-ga
and the
Ice Giants

By David Lee Smith, Thunder Clan

At the beginning of the world, giants roamed the land, battled, and ate human beings. Ma-ona had sent Rabbit down, and he and Turtle had all but cleared the land of the two-legged giants. All that was left were the Ice Giants of the far north, who, as legends say, were created from Ma-ona's tears. These Ice Giants could survive only in cold weather, and they usually journeyed south only in the wintertime, when it was cold and snowy. Then they would circle an Indian village and eat its inhabitants.

One fall, before the snows fell and the journey of the Ice Giants, the Winnebagos celebrated their annual Green Corn dance. This dance was to honor Ma-ona, the Creator, for giving them a wonderful harvest. After the celebration, all Winnebagos traveled back to their villages, to wait and prepare for the coming winter. The village furthest north was ruled by the eldest of the chief's sons. His name was Ku-nu. The second son, Hay-na, was war chief; he controlled the military might of the village. So the brothers Ku-nu and Hay-na were very powerful and everyone paid them respect.

The chief also had a third son called Ha-ga, who had no power whatsoever in the village. His main duty was to take care of the sick and elderly, and he earned a good reputation among the old people for doing this. However, deep in his mind, he wanted to be a warrior. His older brothers never invited him along on the warpath, so he never earned war honors like they did. Nevertheless, the older brothers were

169

very fond of their younger brother and gave him everything he wanted except leadership on the warpath. They did this because of a vow they made to their mother on her deathbed to take care of Ha-ga, the night he was born.

Ha-ga knew that the coming winter would be very cold, because he had seen that his friends the squirrels had thicker fur, and his brothers the bears went to bed too early. So Ha-ga made sure that the old people had enough food and wood to last them through the winter. When all this was done, the third son rested, and laid all other matters in the hands of his elder brothers. Little known to him, the Ice Giants were on their way south.

One morning, Ku-nu went to wake his younger brother Ha-ga for council and found him missing. Ku-nu alerted Hay-na and both searched the whole village and country-side, but they could find no trace of their younger brother. Both felt very bad, for they had broken their vow they made to their mother years before. They and the whole village went into mourning.

Little known to them, the night before, Ha-ga had had a vision from the Creator. Both Rabbit and Turtle came after him and carried him to the upperworld where Ma-ona and the spirit-animals lived. Ma-ona told him that in order to save his people, he had to journey north and battle the Ice Giants before they reached his people's village. The Creator said, "My son, there is nothing I can do to help you, for you must rely on your strength alone." After some time he continued, "For you alone, of all the people I created, can save your people from the Ice Giants that now threaten your village."

After lighting the sacred fires, Ma-ona said, "Years ago I created these ice-beings from my tears to keep the human beings in check from growing too powerful, but now the Ice Giants are too powerful and you must destroy them for me." Ma-ona reached into the fire and pulled out a hot coal. "Take this, my son," Ma-ona said quietly, "for in your darkest hours, it will be your salvation. Listen to your heart, for only your heart will tell you how to use this talisman."

After placing the hot coal in Ha-ga's hand, Ma-ona continued, "Now go, my son, for mortals are not allowed too long in the spirit-lands before their time." Then the whole vision seemed to vanish.

Ha-ga awoke in a cold sweat, for he knew his dream was more than a dream: in his hand he held the talisman that was in the shape of an eagle. After putting the talisman in his belt, Ha-ga went into the night.

Days later, Ha-ga made it to a frozen river, and crossing the frozen river were the Ice Giants. For four days, the battle raged along the river's banks. Every time an Ice Giant fell dead, the whole world shook. But there were too many Ice Giants and Ha-ga knew he was going to lose in the end. His arm was getting tired and his war-ax was getting heavy.

Still, Ha-ga fought on, for he was a Winnebago warrior and he was not afraid. If he was going to die, he would die in battle. After missing an Ice Giant with his ax, Ha-ga was knocked off his feet. Immediately, he began to sing his death-song. This song confused the Ice Giants, giving Ha-ga the time he needed to reach into his belt and bring forth the eagle talisman. Then with a mighty blow, Ha-ga smashed the talisman into a thousand pieces. With that done, the whole northern world seemed to explode. The heavens lit up with a million lights, and the Ice Giants melted into nothingness. Ha-ga fainted.

When he awoke, he was surrounded by two fur-clothed warriors. His brothers had arrived. "Come my brother," Ku-nu said. "We will honor you." When Ha-ga rose to his feet, he said, "No Ku-nu, I cannot accept the honor." "Why not?" asked Hay-na. "You deserve an eagle feather for your bravery." After drinking some water, Ha-ga told them of his vision and the battle with the Ice Giants. "So you see," Ha-ga said, "my power is god-given, and I cannot accept your honor." Deep in his heart, Ha-ga knew he was a warrior. And a true warrior never accepts honor.

The whole northern world lit up once more and all three sons seemed to see their mother smiling at them through the northern lights. After all these years, she finally knew her

Ha-ga was a man, a warrior of her people, and she was glad. Now she returns every winter to melt the Ice Giants who threaten mankind, and gives light to the Winnebago through the long, cold winter.

Folklore
of the
Winnebago
Tribe

The
Chief's Journey
into the Spiritland
to Bring Back His Wife

By David Lee Smith, Thunder Clan

A long, long time ago, when the Winnebagos still lived among the pine trees, there lived a very beautiful woman and her husband, the chief. Everyone in the village liked her. Even the animals and insects liked her, for she was very kind and gentle. One day, the woman became very sick, and this worried her husband a lot. He went out and brought her medicine people to try to make her well. They prepared potions out of herbs for her, but to no avail. She continued to worsen.

So her husband approached a shaman. A shaman is blessed by the spirits. All his powers come from the spirits and Ma-ona himself. The shaman came to see the woman and at once started to pray and sing to her, but again to no avail. She continued to worsen. His chanting went on all night and into the early hours of the morning. The woman died. The husband felt very bad, and he fell into a state of mourning. He cut off his hair.

The shaman alerted the chief's wife's friendship clan—the Bear family, or people with police duty. They immediately came and prepared the body for burial. They washed the woman's body and combed her hair. Then they dressed her in the finest woman's regalia they had. They put new moccasins on her and made a hole in each one. Then they wrapped her in a fur blanket and carried her away to be buried. At the grave site, they prayed and sang the woman's death song and buried her. They placed many things with her so she could use them in the Spiritland.

When this was done, they returned to the village and prepared themselves for the four-nights' wake. They also prepared the feasts they were going to have every day of the wake. At the same time, the husband mourned and prepared a plan in his head. On the morning of the fourth day, at sunrise, a woman from the Bear Clan screamed: this now released the spirit of the dead woman on her journey to the Spiritland. When this was over, they had one more meal and then went home. The only people remaining were the husband and the shaman.

The husband now had a plan. He was going to follow his wife into the Spiritland and try to bring her back. The shaman knew what the man intended to do because of his powers. He said, "My son, there is nothing I can say that will stop you from what you are about to do. You are the chief. I am not." The shaman took a smoke of his pipe and continued, "But now, I will prepare you for what you are about to do." So the shaman prepared a sweat bath for the man. When the rocks were hot, the man entered the sweat lodge and closed the door. The man then dipped sage into a bowl of water and sprinkled the hot rocks with it. This caused steam to be released, and the man started to sweat. At the same time he started to sing. On the outside, the shaman started praying to the spirits for help, so the chief would be successful in his journey.

Early next morning as the sun was about to come up, the shaman led the man out of the sweat house. In each of his hands, he placed four sacred bundles of herbs. They were sweet grass, cedar, sage, and tobacco—the four sacred herbs of Ma-ona, the Creator. He told the chief, "Never let go of these sacred things. If you do, you will never get out of the Spiritland." As the sun lit the eastern horizon, the man walked from the east to the west. (That's how a spirit travels when a person dies: they start out in the east and journey to the west.) The shaman watched the chief until he disappeared and then went to inform the people that the chief had gone on a personal journey.

Four days passed and the man reached a large, flowing river. There was a long log across the water, so the man started walking across it. His walking seemed endless. Then all of a sudden, he heard moaning and crying. He looked around, but could see nothing. So he continued to walk. No sooner had he taken four more steps than he heard the moaning again. He looked down: the moaning was coming from the water. He then knew these were evil spirits. (Only the bad spirits fall into the river; the good spirits make it across the log bridge.) So the man continued his journey and made it across the bridge.

175

The
Chief's
Journey
into the
Spiritland

An old woman was waiting for him there. In her hand she held a war-ax. Her job was to hit the spirit on the head in order to release the spirit on its four-years' journey to the Spiritland. When the old woman saw the chief approaching, she put down her ax and said, "The spirits told me you were coming. Sit down, my grandson, and let us smoke." So they smoked, and she fixed him a bowl of soup to eat. When he was done eating, she told him, "My grandson, you are on a difficult journey. There is nothing I can do to help you. The four spirit-winds will guide you. Never let go of the sacred herbs and always stay on the path. If you leave the path, the evil spirits will get you, and you will never see your wife again." When the man left the old woman, the eastwind helped him along the path laid out for him.

The first year was a long one because every now and then the evil spirits tried to pull him off the path. But he made it. When the first year was drawing to a close, he approached an old man sitting by a small, mat-covered house. This was the northwind. He said, "My grandson, sit down and let us smoke to Ma-ona." After they had smoked, they ate some soup together, which gave the man new energy. After they had prayed together, the man continued his journey to the Spiritland.

The second year was also long. The evil spirits seemed to get worse, but he could feel the presence of the northwind with him, so he prayed and continued on the road of life and death.

At the end of the second year, he again approached another old man sitting by a fire. He knew this was the westwind. The old man said, "Sit down my grandson. You have come a long way, and you must be hungry. But first let us offer up tobacco to Ma-ona." After they had smoked, they ate some soup together, which gave the man new energy. After they had prayed together, the man continued his journey to the Spiritland.

The third year, too, was a very bad year, but whenever the evil spirits tried to pull him off the path, the man could hear the westwind praying and the man made it to the next stop. As before, another old man was waiting for him by a warm fire. This was the southwind, "Sit down, my grandson, and let us offer up food and tobacco to the all-powerful one." After they were done, the old man said, "This is the last year of your journey. If you succeed, you will see your wife again." After smoking some more, he continued, "Never leave the path of life and death, because if you do, you will suffer in the river of evil spirits for a long time. Until the world itself comes to an end." After being wished good luck, the man continued on his journey.

At the middle of the fourth year, the man reached a big mountain range. As he started climbing, the northwind started to blow hard and cold. Every step he took was agony. When he tripped now and then, the southwind would pick him up and place him back on the road of life and death. With the southwind's help, he made it to the top.

The four spirit-winds were waiting for him. Down at the foot of the mountain range was the evil Spiritland. The northwind spoke to him, "Your wife is in the bad Spiritland, because she did something bad in her life. In order to get her out, you will have to go through a very difficult and torturous test, but if you are strong, you will succeed. If not you will suffer until the end of time." The southwind told him, "Never lose your hold on the sacred herbs, and always pray to Ma-ona for strength." So the chief and four spirit-winds continued down the path and into the village.

It was in the early afternoon when the four spirit-winds built the man a small, rush-covered house. They also built him a sweat lodge. After praying and purifying himself, the man sat on a log and waited for evening to come. When the sun disappeared over the western horizon, a drum started beating. The man stood up and followed the four spirit-winds to the center of the village. There there was a large longhouse. They opened the flaps and the man went in and sat on a log that was reserved for him. The drum continued to beat.

177

The
Chief's
Journey
into the
Spiritland

All night long he looked around. He could not see anybody, but he could feel the presence of the evil beings. Every now and then, he could feel people touching him. He closed his eyes and started praying harder. When the sun came up, the drumming stopped, and the presence of the evil beings was gone. The man arose and walked out the door. The four spirit-winds led him back to his rush-covered dwelling.

When the man seated himself, the spirit-winds made him some wild-rice soup. After he ate, he went inside and fell asleep until the early afternoon. When he arose, he took another sweat bath and offered up sweet grass to the Creator. Then the man waited for evening to come around once again. When the sun went down, the drumming started again. The man arose and followed the spirit-winds to the longhouse. Without a word, he went in the door and seated himself on his log.

As the drum continued throughout the night the man looked around, and this time he could see people, but these people had no faces. One by one, they would come over and look at him and laugh aloud from somewhere inside their heads. This went on all night. When the sun came up, the drumming quit and the faceless beings disappeared. Again the man walked to the door and went out. The four spirit-winds led him back to his house.

As before, the spirit-winds prepared him a Winnebago dish. This time, they made buffalo stew for him. After eating, he offered up sage to Ma-ona and went to sleep. As before, he arose in the early afternoon and prepared himself for another sweat bath. After taking a ritual sweat bath, he prayed for courage from Ma-ona. Then he waited. As the sun went down on the third day, he followed the spirit-winds to the center lodge. They quietly opened the flaps, and he went in and sat down.

The drum started beating. As the beat became louder and louder, the evil spirits started to appear. This time they had faces. They were not faces that an ordinary person sees, but faces of the long dead. Some had pieces of meat hanging from their skulls, and some were skeletons. Looking at them was like having your worst nightmare.

Then to the chief's surprise, he saw his wife among them. She was hugging two of the demons. She was still very beautiful, which was odd because she was in the evil Spiritland. She then walked over to him and spit in his face. "What are you doing here?" she asked. "Don't you know I don't want you any more?" The man almost grabbed her, but he held back. She continued, "I am married again. Don't you like my two husbands?"—and she pointed to the two demons. Then she slapped him to make him mad. The man kept calm and continued to pray. Other demons came over and kicked him, knocking him off his log. Some tried to take away his sacred herbs, but his grip was too strong. He picked himself up and resumed his praying. Just as he was about to give up, the sun came up, and the drumming and the evil spirits went away. The man staggered to the door almost worn out and the spirit-winds helped him back to this lodge.

At his house, they made him some vegetable soup to renew his energy. Afterwards, he lay down and went to sleep. In the early afternoon, he arose and took another sweat bath that the spirit-winds had prepared for him. The man offered up sacred cedar to the Creator and waited as before. Soon, in the twilight of the evening, the drum started beating.

Again he arose, but this time the spirit-winds lectured him. The eastwind spoke, "This is going to be the toughest part of your test. In order to survive the night, you need more courage than ever." The westwind also spoke, "If you don't make it through this night, you and your wife will be here forever." Then they led him back to the center lodge and he went in. The place was crowded with evil spirits.

As the drum started picking up the beat, many evil spirits started laughing and taunting him. Some kicked him and scratched him. A couple of times he fell off his log, but he picked himself up and prayed all the harder. Then his wife came over and slapped him until he could feel blood in his mouth. Some of the evil demons pulled his hair out. A couple of times they tried to pull his sacred herbs from his hand. However, the chief was strong, and the evil spirits knew this. They started torturing his wife in front of him. At this point the man almost gave up, but he kept calm and continued to pray. Then as the dawn approached, the evil spirits began to disappear one by one. Some of them were crying, and some went back into the unknown screaming.

As the sun came up in the east, the only two people left in the long-house were the chief and his wife. The man walked over to his wife and hugged her. Then both, carrying each other, walked to the door. The four spirit-winds helped carry them back to the man's lodge. Then as on the last three mornings, the spirit-winds prepared him a Winnebago dish. This time it was deer and corn soup. This immediately renewed the couple's energy. The four winds spoke as one. "You have made it, my grandson, you have won back your wife." Then they offered up tobacco to Ma-ona, the Creator. The four winds continued to speak, "Never again will a Winnebago be allowed in the Spiritland before his time. Only once before has this happened. It was so long ago, but one of your grandfathers returned from the Spiritland with his son." The four spirit-winds led him to the end of the village and disappeared.

The journey back into the real world took four days. As they approached the bridge of life and death, the old grandmother was smiling. "You have done well, my grandson," she said. "You are blessed by Ma-ona himself." Then she raised her ax, and both the man and his wife crossed the bridge back into reality.

As they approached the chief's village they ran into a woman chopping wood. It was the chief's mother. When she saw them, she was terrified because four years earlier her son and disappeared. The son spoke to her, "My Na-ni, it is I, your son and his wife. We have come back to finish our life on this earth as Ma-ona willed." The mother at once grabbed her son and hugged him. The chief continued, "Go out and pick ten women who never knew men. Then go out and pick ten men who never knew women." After drinking some water he said, "We need to prepare a feast for Ma-ona." So the tribe prepared the feast and everyone was happy to have the chief and his wife back. The tribe grew big and prospered.

As the years went by, the chief and his wife grew old together. Then one night, both passed away in their sleep. They found themselves walking hand in hand across the bridge of life and death. But they were happy. The old woman welcomed them into the good Spiritland. It was the only time, they say, that Ma-ona cried. He was welcoming home the two best Winnebagos he ever created.

CPSIA information can be obtained
at www.ICGtesting.com
Printed in the USA
BVHW041803050423
661819BV00002B/56